HOW TO BEAT THE MONEY SHARKS

ROSTERS LTD, LONDON

HOW TO BEAT THE MONEY SHARKS

Wendy Elkington

ROSTERS LTD, LONDON

Published by Rosters Ltd
60 Welbeck St
London, W1

First edition 1988

ISBN 0 948032 32 4

Filmset by Gwynne Printers, Hurstpierpoint, West Sussex
Printed and bound in Great Britain by Cox & Wyman Ltd, Reading

Publication date . . . March 1988.

The facts contained in this book were to the best of the author's knowledge and belief accurate as at the start of March 1988. Readers are urged to take proper professional advice if they are proposing to invest.

Whilst every effort has been made to ensure the accuracy of the information in this book as at the start of March 1988 neither the author or the publishers shall be liable for any errors or omissions.

INTRODUCTION

The idea for this book dates back to the early 1980's when as a journalist on the *Financial Times* I wrote about several scandals where investors had lost part or all of their hard earned savings. This spate of financial swindles led partly to the new investor protection framework which is now being assembled in this country. For the first time investors will have enshrined in law certain financial rights and this book is the first guide to those new rights.

Many people in the City argue that the new laws will codify what is and always has been the best industrial practices but I know from my postbag that all too often those giving advice in the past have failed frequently to match the high standards of practice now being introduced. The new rules will be brought in between April and the summer. I hope How To Beat The Money Sharks will alert investors to their new rights so that armed with this knowledge they will obtain the best service the financial community has to offer.

ROSEMARY BURR
Series editor, March 1988

Contents

CHAPTER ONE: FINDING THE BEST ADVICE

It can take many years of hard labour to build up your financial nest egg. It can take only a few minutes to lose it. A frightening thought indeed. You only have to look at some of the headlines over the last few years to realise that it is all too easy for an unsuspecting investor to fall prey to the money shark. The investment world has become very slick and sophisticated. New laws and financial products seem to spring up every day. Money has become a complex subject. The investor must be on the look out for Jaws!

The present government's policies revolve around financial self sufficiency, and a wide freedom of choice. Home ownership is encouraged and is at its highest ever level. Thanks to privatisation issues, more people than ever before own shares. There are now around 1200 authorised unit trusts. We are all living longer and staying healthier. This means that much more attention must be given to your old age, hence the introduction of new personal pension plans. On the money scene it is definitely all systems go.

One of the most noticeable things about the financial revolution is that there are an incredible number of people trying to sell you financial products. Everybody wants to get in on this very lucrative market. They seem to breed like rabbits. Not only the banks, building societies and insurance companies, but also estate agencies, accountants, brokers of every description and an endless number of investment advisers. Even Marks and Spencer is getting in on the act. It probably won't be too long before the postman will try to sell you a personal accident policy in case you get bitten by a dog!

Investment is largely based on confidence. You do not want to part with your hard earned cash until you are sure you are getting a good deal. Although most forms of investment have some risk element, you want to know that the people you are dealing with are honest and competent. The investor has been crying out for protection from the unscrupulous adviser.

1988 will probably go down in the history books as a landmark for private investors. The year when the regulators finally developed sharp teeth with which to tackle the investment sharks who fed off the general public. The year when the investor was given the legal right to receive a minimum standard of care from his or her investment adviser. The year, also, when investment advisers of all sizes and types up and down the country had to show they were ready, willing and able to regulate themselves within the new statutory framework passed by parliament in the Financial Services Act 1986.

Although the foundations were laid in 1986, it has taken some time for the full structure to take shape. It has not been the easiest of tasks to get the various sides in the financial world to agree on all the points, and the debate still continues. However, from April of this year the most important aspects will be in place with other additions throughout 1988.

Self-regulation

The keynote of the new laws is self regulation. Each section of the world of finance has drawn up a set of rules by which it will be regulated. At the head of it all is the Securities and Investment Board – known as SIB. It is not a government department but it does have far reaching powers. In turn SIB has delegated its authority to various Self Regulatory Organisations – SROs – to cover the five sections. They are:

- AFBD – Association of Future Brokers and Dealers – for firms dealing in financial and commodity futures and options and providing investment management and advice incidental to that business.
- FIMBRA – Financial Intermediaries, Managers and Brokers Regulatory Association for independent intermediaries advising on and arranging deals in investments or providing investment services to clients.
- IMRO – Investment Management Regulatory Organisation – for investment managers and advisers, in

the main institutional fund managers, unit trust and pension fund managers.

- LAUTRO – Life assurance and Unit Trust Regulatory Organisation. It is only concerned with the marketing of life assurance and unit trust products. LAUTRO will not authorise firms to carry on investment business. Unit trust management companies will need to obtain parallel authorisation, probably through FIMBRA, and insurance companies will be authorised by virtue of being recognised under the Insurance Companies Act.
- TSA – The Securities Association, which was formed by the merger of the Stock Exchange with the International Securities Regulatory Organisation. It will cover firms dealing and arranging deals in domestic and international securities plus those advising corporate finance customers.

These organisations cover the whole range of investments, including life policies, pensions, unit trusts, options, futures, debentures, shares, gilts and local authority securities. It excludes general insurance policies, like household, car and holiday cover, bank accounts, and collectors items such as works of art, stamps and coins. What sort of protection is on offer?

Authorisation

- Anyone who wants to operate an investment business now has to be authorised by one of the SRO's. This is a bit like an operating licence and without it a firm cannot do business. Some professional bodies such as the Law Society and the Institute of Chartered Accountants, are treated separately. They have acquired Recognised Professional Body status – or RPB's and can authorise individual members. With these firms, investment advice is incidental to their main business.
- It is a criminal offence to carry on an investment business without a proper authority. Anyone who does faces a prison sentence of up to two years. Any contracts made by an unauthorised firm are not valid.
- People running investment firms have to prove that they are 'fit and proper' before they can be authorised. They must show sound financial resources, a business plan and

capital adequacy. Details of their expertise and experience will be examined. Similarly any complaints made by customers will be investigated and checks made to see if there are any financial judgements or criminal proceedings against the firm and its key people.

Rules of conduct

A crucial part of the Financial Services Act covers the conduct of investment advisers.

1. Customer agreements

You must now be given a written agreement detailing the scope of the services you want. The points to be covered are:

- basic information about the firm
- the type of services to be provided
- information on the cancellation rights of investors in single premium life assurance plans or unit trust plans
- a request by the firm for the right to make unsolicited calls
- a note to say that if this right is given, the investor loses his rights to cancel investments under the fourteen day cooling-off period rule
- the basis, method and frequency of payments must be stated by the firm
- a summary of the advice given and the instructions given by the customer.

2. Client's money rules

Any money held on your behalf must be put in a separate client bank account. Advisers cannot mix the firm's money with the client's money. The audit procedures are designed to ensure that this separation of money is maintained at all times. The money must be placed in an account on trust with a bank approved under the Banking Act 1979. The aim of this rule is to protect investors' cash from being mixed with the company's resources and treated as if it was a company asset.

Some advisors have decided not to handle clients' cash at all and you will be asked instead to make all payments direct to the insurance or unit trust company. From the customer's point of view this further reduces the risk of money going astray, while for the advisor it means they pay a lower fee to the self-regulatory organisation.

Giving advice

From now on, advisers are subject to strict rules when making recommendations. They fall into four areas:

- 'Know the customer'

An adviser must find out all the relevant details which will have a bearing on the investment requirements of the customer. These include the basics such as age, occupation, health, smoker, non smoker and marital status. He should also fully examine the client's financial position, both present and future. Comprehensive records must be kept.

- 'Best Advice'

One of the linchpins of the Financial Services Act. If the adviser represents only one company then he is only expected to know about their products and must act accordingly. However, if he is fully independent, he must examine the entire marketplace and come up with the best recommendations available. He must look at the investment from all angles and from the customer's point of view, not just base his decision on the amount of commission he is likely to earn.

- 'Suitability of Investment'

This follows on quite naturally from the 'best advice' rule. The investment must be appropriate to the customer's particular circumstances. For example, a widow with a limited pension should not be put into a speculative commodity deal.

- 'Polarisation'

This new word has now crept into economic jargon. It means that advisers have to declare exactly where they stand. They must make it totally clear whether they are acting as a representative of a specific company or are totally independent, covering the entire marketplace. No half way house is allowed.

Advertising

The Financial Services Act has brought in new rules on the content of investment advertising, including general mail shots. Clear warnings have to be given about the risks involved in any product. Figures quoted about performance must not be unfairly selective and projections must now be based on standard figures. It should also be made very clear if a particular product is not suitable for a long term investment.

Practical protection

1. Compensation fund

The Securities and Investment Board will operate a compensation fund in case any investor loses money. This should be in operation by July 1988. 100% compensation will be paid for amounts up to £30,000, then 90% on the next £20,000, making a maximum of £48,000. All authorised business may contribute to the fund. There are two important points to bear in mind:

(i) Money is only paid out if an adviser goes bust and cannot meet his debts.

(ii) No money is payable if you lose out because the value of your investments has dropped through normal market forces. All investments carry some form of risk and this should be accepted at the start.

2. Complaints

All investment firms must now have a proper complaints procedure. The details have to be fully investigated and records kept. If you do not get satisfaction from the business involved, you can go direct to the appropriate Self Regulatory Organisation. In addition, you can also complain to the Ombudsman for that particular profession. In a serious case, if the finding is that the complaint is justified, the firm could lose its authorisation and have to stop trading.

3. Cold calling

A cold call is defined in the Financial Services Act as a 'personal visit or oral communication made without an express invitation'. In the past cold calls were permitted on insurance products and investors were protected by being given a ten day cooling off period so that they could change their mind once out of earshot of the persuasive salesman. Under the Act cold calling is being extended to personal pensions and unit trusts. The new rules on cooling off are slightly confusing. There will be a fourteen day cooling off period included in all life assurance and personal pension contracts but a similar cooling off period will only apply to unit trusts sales concluded as a result of a cold call, not all unit trust transactions.

4. Experienced investor
These rules and regulations, enshrined in the Financial Services Act, have been put together to protect the man in the street – who is rather quaintly called the ordinary investor. Different rules apply to the experienced and professional investor. They will obviously know a great deal more about the financial market place and the risks involved in any particular investment. For example, an experienced investor who knows exactly what he wants can opt for 'execution only'. He only expects the broker to carry out his instructions and on that basis the rules of 'best advice' and 'know the customer' do not apply.

Someone said the Financial Services Act came in with a bang but it has been whimpering along ever since. It is a highly complex piece of legislation and has taken much longer to put together than was first thought. It should be regarded more as a prevention than a cure, as it relies on the various organisations weeding out their less desirable members. However, investors can take comfort from the fact that there are now well defined rules in place which should lead to a reduction of some of the past abuses and a higher general standard of service.

Who's Who in investor protection

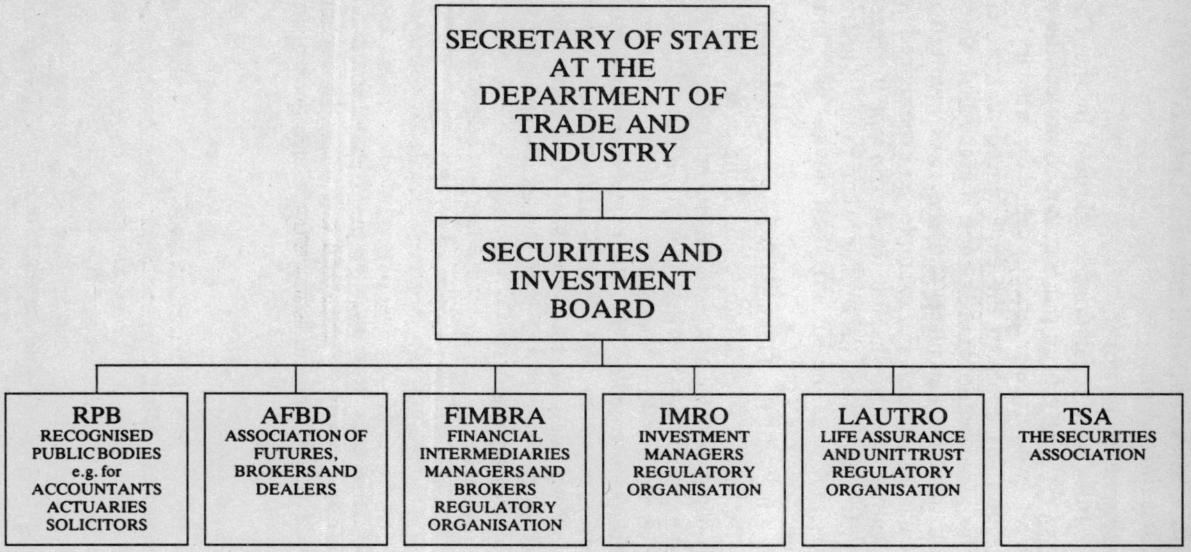

SECRETARY OF STATE AT THE DEPARTMENT OF TRADE AND INDUSTRY
SECURITIES AND INVESTMENT BOARD
RPB
RECOGNISED PUBLIC BODIES e.g. for ACCOUNTANTS ACTUARIES SOLICITORS
AFBD
ASSOCIATION OF FUTURES, BROKERS AND DEALERS
FIMBRA
FINANCIAL INTERMEDIARIES MANAGERS AND BROKERS REGULATORY ORGANISATION
IMRO
INVESTMENT MANAGERS REGULATORY ORGANISATION
LAUTRO
LIFE ASSURANCE AND UNIT TRUST REGULATORY ORGANISATION
TSA
THE SECURITIES ASSOCIATION

CHAPTER TWO: THE HIGH STREET SUPREMOS

Most people start off by asking their bank manager for advice and as he, or in a few cases she, knows your financial affairs this is often a good place to begin. The modern-day bank manager is a bit like a GP, knowing a little bit about a lot of things and referring you to the appropriate specialist when necessary.

Making your choice

Two out of every three bank customers open accounts when they are children or when they start work and stay with the same bank all their lives. The original reasons for choosing a particular bank range from convenient location, family connection through to attractive charges. Now banking is much more competitive and if you are not satisfied with your own bank, the bank next door is keen for your custom. If a bank official can poach a customer from a competitor it's a feather in his – or her – cap. If your business looks likely to be profitable they may even be prepared to under-cut the competitor in terms of costs and conditions. Many charges are made at the manager's discretion which gives customers the chance to negotiate.

Range of advice

Banks provide information and advice on a wide range of money matters. Most have specialist subsidiaries dishing out tax and investment advice to both their domestic customers and expatriates. The days of the traditional bank manager who was heard but not seen are fast disappearing. Under the Financial Services Act the banks had to decide whether they were going to follow the independent route and give impartial advice based on a thorough review of all the products on the market or whether they were simply going to recommend their own in-house bank branded products. Most of the high street banks have decided to only sell their own products with the notable exceptions of National Westminster Bank and the Bank of Scotland. However, most banks have registered their broking subsidiaries as independent and their services will be available to the wealthier private client and corporate customers.

Checking up

If your bank is only recommending its own products, then you should make sure they have a good investment record. The specialist financial magazines like *Money Management* and *Planned Savings* run league tables showing how unit trust and life assurance company funds have performed.

Costs

The first meeting with your bank manager will be free, but if you want a more detailed consultation then you may be charged on a time basis. Make sure you ask in advance the cost of your subsequent visit. The charges will depend on the seniority of the staff, the location of the branch – the West End of London will cost a lot more than the West Country, the financial complexity of your discussions and the work involved.

Limitations

Banks have a reputation for putting customers into conservative investments and usually steer clear of recommending speculative investments.

Bias

Bank branches that have tied agent status will only recommend their own products, so this advice will be biased in their own favour. However, if the branch is registered as an independent adviser, it will recommend products from the whole range available on the market. Make sure you know the status of your own bank. You can ask to be put in touch with the bank's independent broking department if you want broadly based advice.

Safety

The banks are regulated by the Banking Act 1979, which give supervisory power to the Bank of England. There are strict rules governing the conduct of employees. There is a compensation fund which will repay depositors if a bank is in financial difficulties. The fund will pay out a maximum of 75% on deposits rising to £20,000 – so the top limit is £15,000.

Complaints

If you have a complaint about your bank you should take the following steps:

- Write to the local branch manager explaining your grievance.
- Write to the chief general manager at head office. Your local branch will give you the address.
- If this does not work, contact the banking ombudsman, or if the complaint is about an investment problem, try the appropriate self-regulatory association.

BUILDING SOCIETIES

In the past the only thing you would expect to talk to your building society manager about was house purchase or savings accounts. However, from January 1, 1987 societies have been allowed to sell a much wider range of products – shares, unit trusts, pensions and even to offer unsecured loans.

Making your choice

Finding a building society is not a problem. Walk down the main high street in any town and you are bound to see at least one branch office. Building societies have only recently started to train their staff to give all-round financial advice and the quality of that advice varies tremendously. Personal recommendation is still a good way of finding a clued-up building society manager.

Range of advice

Many of the larger building societies are now extending the range of services and products which are available at their branches. Since they are only allowed to devote 10% of their turnover to these new services, most are concentrating on just one or two novel areas. However by 1993 they will be able to devote up to 25% of their turnover on new services.

Checking up

Some societies are planning to be tied agents and offer only one company's products, while others intend to become independent intermediaries giving advice on a wide range of products. Make sure you know into which camp your society falls. If they are selling only one company's products make sure that company has a good investment record.

Costs

So far building societies have not followed in the footsteps of the high street banks in charging a fee for a consultation. They earn commission on any insurance product, unit trusts or shares they sell which rewards their time and effort.

Limitations

Building societies are still pretty new to the investment world and their staff are in the process of being trained to cope with customers' queries. While they should be able to give good advice about mortgages and straightforward savings schemes, many will be less proficient when it comes to intricate tax schemes or specific stock exchange investments. Some have linked up with stockbroking firms, or insurance companies to fill this gap and their staff will call in the experts when you ask for advice on any of these specialist subjects.

Safety

The societies are controlled by the Building Societies Commission Supervisory Body and have to comply with very strict regulations about liquidity ratios, and the services they provide. There is a compensation fund for investors which will pay out up to 90% on investments valued at up to £20,000. Sums in excess of this are not covered. Under the Financial Services Act building societies which give independent investment advice have to be authorised. Virtually all have asked for authorisation from the Securities and Investment Board, which means among other things that any complaints will be investigated by the board's independent investigator.

Some building societies have decided to become tied agents, i.e. simply sell the investment products of one company. In such cases if you have any complaints go direct to the investment company concerned.

Building societies are exempt from the compensation arrangements set up under the Financial Services Act so customers have to rely on their protection under the existing compensation fund.

Complaints

If you have a complaint about your building society you should take the following steps:

- Talk to the branch manager.
- Write to the chief executive at the society's head office.
- Write to the building society ombudsman, or if it is an investment problem the appropriate self-regulatory association, which is likely to be the Securities and Investment Board.

MERCHANT & INVESTMENT BANKS

A new association called the British Merchant Banking and Securities Houses Association was formed in January 1988. It was formed by a merger of the Accepting Houses Committee and the Issuing Houses Association.

Its members include all the old 'merchant' banks and many others as well – probably a total of 80. Many offer investment management service for private clients with assets of around £100,000 or more. Some offer a packaged service for less wealthy customers, but most will simply channel their savings into the bank's in-house funds.

Making your choice

The best way of finding a good adviser is through personal recommendation. If that does not work, write to three or four and interview them to see what range of services they offer.

Range of advice

Most banks restrict their service to portfolio management, although they will liaise with your accountant on tax matters and your solicitor if legal problems crop up. They will invest your money in shares, gilts and cash deposits and in addition might recommend investments such as BES schemes. Many have good contacts overseas and so are well placed to advise you on investment opportunities in the major world markets like New York, Tokyo and the European markets.

Portfolios are individually structured to meet your particular requirements and a manager is usually assigned to each account. The manager will give general financial advice and may suggest appropriate expert help where necessary. The accent is very much on a tailor-made approach for high-income clients or customers with plenty of assets.

Checking up

Not all the banks have a top-notch investment record and it is worth looking at their 'shop window investments' such as unit trusts and pensions to see how they have performed relative to other groups.

Costs

The fee scales vary a lot from bank to bank. Most have a minimum annual charge, usually in the region of £500 to £750, and then charge dealing costs on share transactions. Normally, the fee is calculated on a percentage basis such as 1% of the assets under management. Some banks will take clients either on a discretionary basis or an advisory basis and may well charge a higher fee for the latter as it is more time-consuming. Always check out the total fees charged.

Limitations

The likelihood is that some of your cash will end up invested in in-house funds – perhaps for the overseas content. These banks are biased towards stock exchange investments which have a high risk profile, but over the long term should prove rewarding.

Safety

These banks are tightly regulated by the Bank of England and their affairs are closely monitored. In addition, they are required under the Financial Services Act to register with the appropriate self-regulatory organisation which in most cases will be IMRO – the Investment Managers Regulatory Organisation. They will be covered by the Financial Services Compensation Manager Ltd, which means if they become insolvent you are entitled to receive 100% of any investments up to £30,000 and 90% of investments up to £20,000.

Complaints

If you have a problem over the management of your account take the following steps:

- Talk to your portfolio manager
- Write to the chief executive of the bank
- Write to the Bank of England or the appropriate self-regulatory association.

CHAPTER THREE: DEFUSING THE SALESMEN

"Can I ask you a few questions, I'm conducting a survey" is one of the more popular opening gambits favoured by the clip-board merchants. Basically they are trying to sell you an investment, usually life assurance. They are to be found not only on the streets, but also knocking on your front door.

Cold-calling is the name of the game – these people are trying to sell you something and to ensure you listen to them, they will not reveal their real intention until they think you are well and truly hooked. The Securities and Investment Board defines cold-calling as a personal visit or oral communication made without your express prior request.

The clip-board merchants usually work for what can loosely be described as 'financial services companies', often insurance companies with uncompetitive products.

New rights

You now have more protection than ever before against that smooth talking money shark plugging his financial wares on your doorstep. You still need to be on your guard, however, as you could find that even though you can change your mind and cancel an investment you will be the poorer for it. This rule applies to unit trust sales made as a result of an unsolicited or cold call. Under the new rules you can cancel the deal within fourteen days but, a big but, if the value of the units has fallen in the meantime you suffer the loss. So for example if the rules had been in place last October and you had been persuaded to buy shares in a UK unit trust by a doorstepping salesman the week before the share crash on October 19 and you then wanted to cancel the deal you could have suffered a 25% loss of your money. Incidentally if the units rise in value you do not receive any of this profit.

Those buying insurance products or personal pensions will find themselves better off since the cooling off period is being extended from ten to fourteen days. Since your money is not invested straight away the problems over short term market swings experienced on the unit trust side do not come into play.

Perhaps the major plus for the customer is that salesmen will have to come clean and reveal their true purpose. It will be illegal to use the "I'm conducting a survey" gambit. They will also have to tell you whether they are representing a single company or offering independent advice.

Range of advice

While salesmen from large reputable companies will be able to help you plan your investment and savings strategy, and recommend a product from his or her company, clip-board merchants often represent small companies whose training technique may leave something to be desired. To obtain advice about comparative products from other companies you would need to consult an independent broker.

Charges

You will not have to pay these salesmen anything. They earn commission on each sale from the company whose products they are marketing.

Safety

While it is illegal for salesmen not to 'reveal' their identity immediately, it is hard to believe that all will conform to this rule. So here are some tips about coping with smooth talking salesmen:

- If the salesman does not immediately say who he or she is working for, ask. Ring up the company and say that their salesman failed to identify him or herself. If the firm does not seem concerned then contact the Securities and Investment Board.
- Do not be taken in by opening lines about surveys – real market researchers carry identification with the name of their company and a photograph of the researcher. Always ask to see any identification card. Never let strangers into

your home or give them information about when you will be home.

- If you are rung up by a researcher, and want to answer the questions, but are unsure whether it is a bona fide call – ask for their number and ring them back.
- If you are really interested in life assurance or unit trusts, ask them to send you their literature. Shop around, consult other advisers and compare the costs and benefits.
- If you fall victim to a smooth talking salesman, remember that you have a fourteen day cooling off period during which you are perfectly free to change your mind about any insurance product. If you have any doubt at all, cancel the policy straightaway. After the cooling off period has lapsed you stand to lose a large chunk of your cash if you cancel the investment in the early years of its life.

Complaints

- Write to the managing director of the company whose products they are selling.
- Write to the Securities and Investment Board or the appropriate self-regulatory association.

COMPANY REPRESENTATIVES

When the new rules contained in the Financial Services Act all come into force anyone selling life assurance will have the choice of:

- registering as an independent intermediary
- becoming an appointed representative
- becoming a company representative

An appointed representative is a firm of investment advisers whose members are authorised to give advice and sell the products of one company or group only. An individual who is allowed to sell the products and services of one company or group only is referred to as a company representative. Both categories must make it clear to clients that they only work for a single company. All promotional material which they use, including their headed notepaper must make this fact clear. Under the new act it is a criminal offence for a company representative to place investment business with any company other than the one which they have chosen to represent.

Quality of advice

Most companies put salesmen through a rigorous training programme. Usually the salesmen start by selling only the most basic products and refer inquiries on more complex subjects to more experienced colleagues. They are progressively allowed to sell a wider range of products with normally only experienced salesmen being permitted to sell complex risky investments.

Under the new regulations, companies have to ensure their salesmen are technically competent to sell their products. They have to adhere to a strict code of conduct and must follow the 'best advice' and 'know your customer' rules laid down in the Financial Services Act. This means they are under an obligation to recommend the best products for the investor from the product range of their own company. They must also advise customers if their company has no suitable contract to meet their needs.

The company representative must take into account all the customer's known financial circumstances in giving advice. This includes things like income, outgoings, existing policies. He or she must provide the customer with full product information including details on the investment linked charges, likely return to the policyholder on early surrender, the purpose and nature of the product.

Cost

The point to remember about salesmen is that they are often self-employed and paid on results. They earn commission based on the products they sell. Some policies, like life assurance bonds, pay a higher commission level than others, like unit trusts. The salesman is not bound to disclose how much commission he or she will be earning by selling you any particular scheme unless you ask or if the company is paying a higher than standard rate of commission. The commission is included in the price of the product regardless usually of whether you buy it through a salesman, independent adviser or direct.

Identifying the salesman

The salesmen must carry a business card with his or her name and the company's name. Some companies issue their salesmen with photo-cards which makes identification even easier.

Cooling off

At the moment, if you buy an insurance product as a result of an unsolicited or a 'cold call' then you can cancel it within ten days and obtain a full refund of your money. Under the new regulations, there is a fourteen-day cooling off period for all investment products including unit trusts, life assurance plans and pensions. The new cooling-off period applies to all sales made on or after July 1, whether they are made subsequent to a cold-call or any other method. The exception is unit trusts where the fourteen-day cooling off period only applies after a cold-call. A golden rule is that when paying, always do so by cheque, never in cash, as this guarantees a record of payment. Always make out the cheque to the company, never the salesman.

If you think you may have been sold the wrong sort of product, or have a problem, get in touch with the salesman's branch office. Companies should ensure that members of the public do not suffer financially in the event of any misdeeds on the part of their salesmen. Such companies will have a fidelity bond, a form of insurance which provides cover in the event of dishonesty by a sales associate. You can always ask the sales representative whether his or her company does have such a policy.

Safety

If you are sold an insurance product and the insurance company goes bust, then under the Policyholders Protection Act you will receive up to 90% of your entitlement. This act only covers authorised UK insurance companies, not offshore firms.

Complaints

- Contact the branch office
- Write to the managing director at the head office

- If the company belongs to the Insurance Ombudsman scheme or the Personal Insurance Arbitration Service write explaining your problem
- If it is an investment problem, contact either the organisation which gave it authorisation, or if the company does not participate in this scheme you will have to rely on SIB's investigation department

INDEPENDENT ADVISERS

Anyone offering independent financial advice on 'investments' – pensions, life assurance and shares, will have to be authorised to do so. They can get authorisation from the Securities Investment Board directly or from one of the self-regulatory organisations. Most intermediaries are likely to register with the Financial Intermediaries, Managers, Brokers Regulatory Association, but those firms who manage Stock Exchange investments may prefer to register with the Investment Managers Regulatory Organisation. Some brokers who do not wish to handle clients' money and who only arrange a limited amount of investment business (maximum of 25% of their total) are registered with the Insurance Brokers Registration Council which has 'Recognised Professional Body' status.

Making your choice

Once again, the best way is through personal recommendation. Failing that you can ask the Financial Intermediaries, Managers, Brokers Regulatory Association for lists of their members and contact local firms.

British Insurance & Investment Brokers Association – BIIBA also has lists of its members.

FIMBRA

The members are divided into different categories depending on the sort of business they do. The basic type of membership will cover such things as life policies, unit trusts and pensions. However there is an important distinction to make. Some advisers are not allowed to handle clients' money. Cheques should therefore be made payable direct to the company whose products you are buying, not the adviser. Other firms will be authorised to handle clients cash, but they must keep it in a separate bank account. Large firms can handle a wider range of investments, sometimes on a discretionary basis. Again there is a distinction between those who can handle money and those who cannot.

People who now operate under labels such as insurance broker, adviser, consultant, mortgage broker, unit trust broker, licensed dealer will have to obtain authorisation. The titles they will use in future will include: investment broker, investment manager, collective investment intermediary, investment adviser and investment dealer. However, as loans are not covered by the Financial Services Act (1986) advice from a mortgage broker about the way to arrange your mortgage does not fall within the requirement of the best advice rule. However, recommendations on the comparative merits of various endowment mortgages is covered.

Range of advice

They cover a broad spectrum of savings and investment schemes, including unit trusts and insurance products, pensions and share transactions. Under the Financial Services Act advisers must recommend the products best suited to their client's needs, taking into account all their own personal financial circumstances.

Checking up

As advisers in this category do not have instantly recognizable 'professional status' it is essential to check them over very carefully.

- All firms have to be authorised, many by FIMBRA. If you are in any doubt, you can always ask for the authorisation number and check it out with that organisation. Fimbra members are allowed to display a distinctive logo once they are authorised.

- An adviser cannot pretent to do a wider range of business than the ones he has been authorised to carry out. You can always ask for his business description. This will show full details, including whether or not he can handle clients' cash.

- Under the Financial Services Act, investment advisers are not forced to take out professional indemnity insurance. However, many of the good ones do have this extra cover and you should check this.

- Have a chat with the adviser to see if you feel comfortable with the approach.

Beware of advisers who ask a few cursory questions and only seem interested in getting your money – the alarm bells should start ringing. Check their range of expertise by asking about gilts, national savings, building societies. Ask the adviser about his or her background, how long they have been in the business, what qualifications they have and what they did before joining the firm.

Do not be impressed by plush offices and flash cars, remember at the end of the day it is their clients who paid for these luxuries. Look for membership of one of the associations which will guarantee your adviser meets certain standards. The following are best known:

- British Insurance and Investment Brokers Association
  A trade association with over 4,000 members. It is the largest and best known trade body and its members include the 'mega brokers' as well as the small one-man-band brokers. It has a disciplinary body, a complaints procedure and members must have professional indemnity insurance.

- Corporation of Insurance and Financial Advisers
  It was formed in 1968 to combat the spate of rogue mortgage broking and has grown rapidly. Now the foremost body in the field of mortgage broking. Each member has to have professional indemnity and there is a disciplinary committee.

- Institute of Insurance Consultants
  This aims to enhance the status and ethical standards of insurance consultants. It has around 3,000 members and will act as an arbitrator in disputes between members and act on behalf of a member in disputes with others. There is a strict code of conduct to which members must adhere and a complaints and disciplinary committee meets regularly to look at problems. Members must have professional indemnity insurance to a minimum level which is adequate to the requirements of their level of business.

LICENSED DEALERS

Licensed dealers used to be licensed by the Department of Trade and Industry, but now they come under the Financial Services Act rules. They have to be authorised by a self regulatory organisation – usually FIMBRA. They will buy and sell shares in a limited range of companies. They will advertise that they can sell your British Gas, British Airways shares for you at a cut-price fee or even free. While on the surface their offers look attractive, you usually find the fee is simply rolled up into the price. In addition, after you have dealt with them once they will put your name on a dealing list and you will get regular mailing shots highlighting the attractions of other shares. Treat these tips with great caution and always get a second opinion before dealing.

These companies often specialise in shares which are traded on the over-the-counter market. If you are tempted to buy check to see whether the shares will be as easy to sell. With over-the-counter shares you run the risk that you may be put into a 'selling queue' which could last days, months or even forever. Licensed dealers do not have to pass the stringent exams which stockbrokers have to take – and do not have the same strict code of conduct as does the Stock Exchange.

Costs

Some advisers will charge fees, others will collect commissions from the companies whose products they are selling. Always find out what charges are involved before handing over your money.

Limitations

Advisers tend to specialise in one area – life assurance, unit trusts, or whatever. Make sure you know what your firm's speciality is and do not expect wide ranging advice. Never be afraid to ask for a second opinion.

Safety

From the 1st July, 1988 customers will be protected by the compensation fund set up under the Financial Services Act. This covers investments up to £48,000 in the event of the dealer being unable to meet his debts and going into liquidation. Until then there is no cover unless the dealer has some form of professional indemnity insurance.

Complaints

If you are unhappy about your adviser's performance take the following steps:

- Take up the matter with the adviser
- Write to the senior partner of the firm
- Write to the appropriate professional body or the people who gave the company its licence or authorisation.

INSURANCE BROKERS

Insurance brokers come in all the shades of the rainbow. They range from the large Lloyds brokers, who insure ships and aeroplanes worth millions of pounds, to the small family-orientated broker who can insure you, your valuables and your home.

Making your choice

If your friends cannot recommend someone then write to the British Insurance and Investment Brokers Association which will send you names of brokers in your area willing to take on new business. FIMBRA also keeps member lists. Alternativcly you can look in the 'Yellow Pages' and choose names at random and ring them up.

Range of advice

Most advisers who deal with personal customers cover both life assurance and general insurance business. They must stick to the 'know your customer' rule when giving advice on life assurance and unit trusts. This means that they must give advice which takes into account your financial circumstances. They must look at your income, outgoings, the purpose of the insurance and any existing policies you have before making recommendation.

Checking up

Anyone who calls him or herself an insurance broker must be registered with the Insurance Brokers Registration Council (IBRC). Before they can register, they have to meet the council's standards. There is a disciplinary committee which meets regularly to look at complaints. It lays down a strict code of conduct which members must follow. Brokers must have professional indemnity cover, but following changes announced early in 1987 they no longer need cover against fraud and dishonesty of directors and partners. However, they do require cover against employee fraud and dishonesty.

The IBRC has a grant scheme, which compensates policyholders in the event of broker fraud or negligence. This is financed by contributions from registered brokers, but the council hopes in future to raise an annual levy on all registered brokers in order to fund the scheme.

Most brokers dealing in life assurance and pensions business will register with the Financial Intermediaries, Managers, Brokers Regulatory Association. If your insurance man calls himself an adviser or consultant – he won't be registered with the IBRC but could be a member of either the Corporation of Insurance and Financial Advisers or the Institute of Insurance Consultants, both of whom have disciplinary schemes.

Costs

Insurance advisers do not charge a fee – they get paid commission by the insurance company whose products they sell. New commission rates have been set up by the Life Assurance Unit Trust Regulatory Organisation and companies paying commission to independent intermediaries have two choices:

1. Never paying more than the standard scale to any broker.
2. Exceeding the standard scale in some or all cases.

When a broker sells a product of a company which falls into category one all you need to be told is that the adviser is receiving the standard scale of commission. However, if you ask the broker how much commission is payable they have to tell you. In case number two the actual amount of commission paid must be disclosed at the outset. The vast majority of companies have decided to pay only standard commission rates.

Limitations

Insurance advisers usually restrict their advice to indirect investments and package deals rather than individual shares and stocks. Many are not investment specialists and rely on briefings from insurance companies, stockbrokers and unit trust managers. Their advice is geared towards insurance policies and few claim to provide an all-round investment service.

Safety

Most insurance advisers carry professional indemnity insurance so this will pay up in the event of fraud or negligence. There will be a compensation fund for all members of self-regulatory organisations by July of 1988 but it only pays out if the broker goes into liquidation. If in doubt about a broker, ask which professional body they belong to and check the current status of their membership.

Complaints

If you have a complaint about your broker take the following steps:

- Write to the broker.
- Write to the senior partner in the firm.
- Write to the appropriate self regulatory body.
- You can contact BIIBA, the trade body for brokers and ask them to investigate the complaint. BIIBA carries out a conciliation service and will look into a wider range of complaints than the self-regulatory association.

CHAPTER FOUR: COPING WITH THE PROFESSIONALS

Anyone can call themselves an accountant. So it is essential to make sure the person you choose is properly qualified and a member of a recognised professional body.

Making your choice

The best way to pick an accountant is undoubtedly by personal recommendation. A firm that has looked after friends or business colleagues well is likely to give you good services too. Alternatively, you can look through the yellow pages, the Thomson Local Directory or write to one of the professional bodies below asking for a list of their members who practice in your locality.

When you are looking for an accountant, check that he or she is properly qualified and specialises in the area in which you need help. There are a number of professional accountancy bodies in this country:

- The Institute of Chartered Accountants in England and Wales
- The Institute of Chartered Accountants in Scotland
- The Association of Certified Accountants
- The Chartered Institute of Management Accountants
- The Chartered Institute of Public Finance and Accountancy
- The Institute of Chartered Secretaries and Administrators

A properly qualified accountant will have initials after his or her name showing the association he or she belongs to. If in any doubt you can always ring the association's head office to make sure you will be dealing with a member in good standing. Members of the Institute of Chartered Accountants are called 'Chartered Accountants' and of the Association 'Certified Accountants'.

Range of advice

Accountant's advice for individuals tends to be limited to tax planning, though a growing number of firms now offer a comprehensive investment advice service as well. The majority still steer clear of giving specific advice, but are often excellent sources of assistance on overall planning.

If you run your own business, or are self-employed an accountant is essential. Not only will he or she be able to advise you on taxation, VAT and corporate planning, but they will give you useful tips on cost control, cash flow, management accounts and controls. Their fees can be offset against any profits you make.

Accountants are also very useful if you have sizeable sums to invest and need to consider the tax implications carefully. They can also give tips on saving for retirement, wills and trusts.

Checking up

Draw up a short list of two or three accountants within easy distance and visit them. Find out about their experience in the field you need advice on, the range of their services and their fees.

Costs

Always ask in advance what fees your accountant will charge. These will vary depending upon the size and location of the firm as well as the seniority of the staff involved. Current fees range from about £20 up to £100 an hour. If an accountant sells you an insurance or pension plan then you should expect them to reduce your fees by the amount of commission they earn. If this does not happen automatically, insist they do so.

Limitations

Under the terms of the Financial Services Act accountants who want to give investment advice can seek authorisation from their own professional body provided that they do not earn more than 20% of their gross fee income from investment business. Any accountant who wants to do a larger percentage of investment business than this must seek authorisation from a self-regulatory organisation – normally FIMBRA.

Accountants can either set up as an authorised investment business or liaise with an authorised independent intermediary and refer clients to them. Their professional body does not allow them to become tied agents to just one company.

Safety

A properly qualified accountant is required to adhere to strict rules laid down by his or her professional association. However, there is nothing to stop them practising even if they have been thrown out of their professional association. Most have professional indemnity insurance, so if their advice proves faulty and you sue, the insurance company will settle for the accountant. Under the Financial Services Act if they want to give investment advice they must be authorised.

Complaints

If you have a complaint about your accountant you should take the following steps:

- Take the matter up with the accountant handling your affairs.
- Write a letter to the senior partner of the firm stating the facts and figures.
- If you still feel dissatisfied write to the accountant's professional body. Normally this will be displayed on the firm's letterhead, but you can always ring up and ask for it. When writing make sure you give as much relevant information as possible, including photostats of any letters or documents relating to the case.
- If the complaint concerns investment advice contact the accountant's professional body and ask for it to be investigated.
- If it concerns a straightforward accounting matter then if you are not satisfied with the response from the professional body you should seek redress via the courts as none of the accountancy associations can award you compensation.

Each association has its own disciplinary codes to which members are bound to adhere, and a complaints procedure. By far the largest association, the Institute of Chartered

Accountants, has an investigation committee which will investigate complaints. They take evidence from both sides and decide what action, if any, is necessary. They may impose sanctions, fines or insist that the accountant takes 'practitioner sessions' to improve their overall knowledge. Their ultimate sanction is expulsion. In 1987 the institute expelled eight members and disciplined a further sixty-four. If your case falls into this category of 'public concern' then it will be investigated by the Joint Disciplinary Scheme which is run by the three main accountancy bodies.

SOLICITORS

Now that solicitors no longer have a monopoly over conveyancing, they are increasing their range of activities and a number now offer a financial advice service to clients.

Making your choice

As with an accountant, the best way of finding a solicitor is through personal recommendation. Failing that try your local Citizens Advice Bureau and ask if they can recommend someone. Most Citizens Advice Bureaux, libraries and law centres should stock a copy of the 'Solicitors Regional Directory', published by the Law Society, which lists all the law firms in a specific area and the type of work they are prepared to conduct. Solicitors must be fully qualified in order to practise. If you want to make sure the solicitor is in good standing you can check with the Law Society.

Range of advice

Solicitors are not trained investment experts and used to limit their advice on personal matters to housing, wills and insurance matters. However, an increasing number are now beginning to give financial advice on a wider range of subjects. Under the terms of the Financial Services Act, solicitors can obtain authorisation from their professional body, the Law Society, provided their gross income derived from investment business does not exceed 20% of their total earnings. If the investment business does exceed 20%, then they must seek authorisation from a self-regulatory organisation – normally FIMBRA.

The Law Society does not allow its members to become tied agents and so solicitors have a choice of either setting up as independent financial advisers or liaising with an authorised independent intermediary and referring clients to him.

Checking up

A good solicitor will be a busy solicitor – unless he or she is new to the practice. So when you go for your initial meeting you should be able to judge the size of the practice.

Costs

Solicitors' fees are calculated on a time basis and will vary depending on the location of the firm. Law firms based in London are probably the most expensive in the country and those in small village the least expensive. The size of the fee will also depend on the seniority of the person handling your case. As a rough guide, expect to pay around £30 an hour, if you are talking to a junior in a London firm or a senior provincial solicitor, and £100 plus if you are talking to a senior partner in a large London firm.

Always check the fees before you start to avoid any unpleasant shocks later on. If a solicitor arranges a life assurance policy or pension plan, they should offset the commission they earn against their fees. If they do not offer to do this – ask.

Safety

Solicitors have to comply with the rules and regulations laid down by the Law Society. The Law Society is a recognised public body and can authorise its members to do investment business. It will investigate complaints.

Complaints

If you have a complaint about your solicitor take the following steps:

- Write to the solicitor.
- Write to the senior partner of the firm.
- Contact the Solicitors' Complaints Bureau.

ESTATE AGENTS

These days your friendly estate agent will not only sell you a house, but also arrange your mortgage and suggest a savings plan in the unlikely event of you having any spare cash. Estate agents have been transformed over the last couple of years and many are now subsidiaries of the largest banks, insurance companies and building societies in the country.

Making your choice

Word of mouth is usually the best way to find an estate agent. If you are buying you should get on all the local agents' lists to be sent details of suitable properties. If you are selling, talk to several to see how much they think your property is worth and what commission they will charge.

Check to see whether the agent has any professional qualifications. This is particularly important if you are asking an agent to survey or value your property. The top name in the business is the Royal Institute of Chartered Surveyors. It has a strict code of conduct to which all members must adhere and a disciplinary scheme if they step out of line.

The Incorporated Society of Valuers and Auctioneers also operates a strict code of conduct. The newest association is the National Association of Estate Agents. All three insist that their members carry professional indemnity insurance to protect clients' money. Do not hand over a deposit to an agent unless they have adequate indemnity cover.

Range of advice

Estate agents are increasingly becoming involved in the investment business. In the past they only advised on mortgages – but many try and sell you a pension or savings scheme and talk to you about life cover. The big chains of estate agencies are in the main owned by banks and insurance companies and all these firms have opted to sell only their own group's products. The main exception is the Nationwide Anglia chain which has chosen the independent route and has applied to the Securities and Investment Board for authorisation.

Many of the small agencies have opted for 'tied agent' status – so they will only be recommending the products of one company. Others are operating what is known as the 'conduit' – they pass customers on to authorised independent financial advisers. If your agent is a company representative – make sure the products he is selling have a good reputation before you sign up.

Checking up

If you want to check an estate agent's credentials, say for example, you are having a full structural survey and want to make sure the agent is properly qualified then ask which, if any, professional association they belong to. It should be mentioned on the letterhead and on the sales particulars. You can ring up the association to make sure he or she is a member in good standing. Alternatively you can write to one of the professional associations and ask for a list of their members in your area.

Costs

Estate agents' commission varies enormously, depending on which part of the country you are trying to sell a property. In London, you usually have to pay between 2% and 3% – but in the provinces you might find the cost a full percentage point lower. Always try and negotiate on the commission charge. Agents may be tempted to accept a lower rate than the one they first suggest, particularly if business is slack.

The points to check are: whether or not advertising costs are covered, whether indeed the agent will advertise the property and are there any extra charges for boards, printing up details of the house or showing clients around.

Limitations

Estate agents earn their living by selling a property. Financial advice, in the main, is limited to mortgages. As they will earn more commission by arranging an insurance-linked mortgage than a straight repayment mortgage, they will usually recommend the former. However, the return on insurance policies varies tremendously depending on the manager's skill and overall investment conditions, so always ask about the investment background of the company which will be managing your money.

Safety

All estate agents are required by law to keep house buyers' deposits in a 'client account'. If you are handing over any money to an agent, you should find out whether or not they have professional indemnity insurance. If you are suspicious, ask to see the certificate. Agents often ask for a deposit when you first make an offer on a house. Legally you do not have to give one – it is just an indication of your good faith.

Complaints

If you have a complaint about an estate agent you should take the following steps:

- Take up the complaint with the agent handling your affairs.
- Write to the senior partner of the firm.
- Write to the professional body to which the agent belongs – or to the parent company if the agency is owed by one of the mega-financial institutions.
- If you are unhappy about any investment advice given write to the body which authorised the agent in the first place. Under the Financial Services Act all such regulatory associations must provide effective and independent channels of investigation.

The Royal Institution of Chartered Surveyors will investigate complaints alleging unprofessional conduct over a wide field including unjustified delays, and disclosure of confidential information. It cannot investigate complaints where the law provides a remedy such as negligence claims, nor can it assess or award compensation. If you have a complaint where there is legal redress you should consult a solicitor or talk to your local Citizens Advice Bureau.

STOCKBROKERS

You can write to the Stock Exchange and they will recommend brokers in your area who are prepared to take on new private clients. The Stock Exchange will also send you a free booklet called 'An introduction to the stock market' which lists all member firms, so you could select a couple who are conveniently located for you and ring them up to arrange an interview. Only advisers who have passed the Stock Exchange exams can call themselves stockbrokers.

Traditionally stockbrokers concentrated on stocks, shares and gilt-edged securities. However, many firms are now building up a fully fledged investment service as well and will give advice on all aspects of the investment business.

Checking up

If you found your broker through a friend, ask about the quality of the advice. Alternatively you can ask to see some of the research the firm has recently produced and can check to see how good this has proved to be by looking at the price of the shares today compared to when they were recommended.

Costs

Stockbrokers earn their living from commissions when shares are bought or sold. Brokers will normally take on clients on one of three bases, and the charges you pay will depend on which service you opt for.

At the bottom of the charges scale is the no-frills dealing only service. The broker will take your order to buy or sell shares and execute it, but will not give you any advice. The minimum charge ranges from £10 upwards in the provinces up to £15 to £30 in London. There are now share shops in department stores, in some building societies and some bank branches – and all offer the same no-frills approach. If you want your investments looked after by a professional, you should ask for a discretionary service. Normally you have to have assets worth at least £20,000 for a London firm to consider your business. Discretionary portfolios are charged commission – typically 1.65% on orders worth up to £7,000 and then 0.55 or 0.5% on larger amounts, though one or two firms drop the commission to just 0.35% on orders worth a quarter of a million or more.

Some brokers charge discretionary clients an annual management fee as well as any transaction charges. The current trend is for brokers to give clients the choice of choosing beween a fixed flat fee or one where any commissions generated beyond a certain level can be used to offset the flat charge.

If you want to have a say in how your money is invested, then you need an advisory service. Here again you will pay a dealing charge and sometimes a flat fee as well, typically around £75 a year. Provincial brokers nearly always charge lower fees than their City competitors. The share shops are often expensive as they have high overheads to cover.

Safety

Stockbrokers are strictly regulated by the Stock Exchange, have to pass stiff exams before they can practise as a broker and must adhere to a rigorous code of conduct. The compensation fund now in existence pays out £250,000 per client and up to £500,000 if securities go missing.

Complaints

If you are not satisfied with your broker's action you should take the following steps:

- Tell the broker that you are unhappy and see if he/she will put matters right.
- If he will not budge, then write to the senior partner of his firm.
- If you are still dissatisfied, you can write to the Enforcement Division of The Securities Association. Explain clearly the nature of the problem and enclose details of any relevant paperwork. Your complaint will be investigated thoroughly.

CHAPTER FIVE: GETTING THE WATCHDOGS TO BARK

When things go wrong in the money world they can hit your pocket and your lifestyle very hard. So where can you turn if either you do not wish or cannot afford to take your case to court? It all depends upon the subject of your complaint and whether the company you are doing business with is covered by one of the growing number of industry watchdogs.

There are three basic types of watchdog up and growling:

- Ombudsman schemes

These are impartial referees who act rather like a judge sitting alone without a jury. He or she usually has some legal training and is an independent appointee. At present there are three government ombudsman and three industry ombudsman. They do not usually charge fees and they can order the company involved in any misdeed to pay you compensation and restore you to the position you should have been in. They act as a supplement rather than a replacement for court action giving aggrieved consumers another route through which to pursue their claim.

- Arbitration schemes

Here an independent arbitrator decides the rights or wrongs of your case and gives a verdict which is binding on both parties. From the consumer's point of view this process is often less satisfactory than an ombudsman as it involves giving up your legal right of redress through the courts and there may be a ceiling on the sum of compensation you can receive. However, it is legally binding on both parties so the company cannot wriggle out of any order to compensate you made by the arbitrator.

- Independent investigators under the umbrella of a self-regulatory or professional body

Under the terms of the Financial Services Act anyone giving

investment advice must be authorised either by a self-regulatory organisation or the Securities and Investment Board. Each self-regulatory organisation must provide what is described in the act as an effective and independent investigation procedure as well as participating in a compensation fund. There is no power under the act to insist that member companies are bound by the decisions of such investigations, although some self-regulatory organisations may build this feature into their schemes and the Securities and Investment Board will keep a watchful eye to see that all authorised companies conduct themselves properly.

Banking ombudsman

In 1986, the high street banks set up an ombudsman scheme and a strong committee including public figures like trade union leaders and consumer champions to see the scheme was run fairly. All the clearing banks belong to the scheme, the first banking ombudsman started operating in January 1986 with power to take decisions on cases which occurred in or after January 1986, i.e. complaints about lending decisions, anything relating to company accounts or interest rate policies. The ombudsman can only start looking at complaints if you have failed to obtain satisfaction through the bank's own complaints procedure.

Areas covered

The most frequent complaints raised are over disputed withdrawals from cash machines, bank charges, negligence, unauthorised debits, executor and trusteeship matters, mortgage loan accounts and problems when closing an account.

Powers

The ombudsman has powers to order the bank involved to pay compensation of up to £50,000, or £100,000 if the complaint was about an event happening on or after January 25, 1988. The decision is binding on the bank, but the individual is free to disregard it and take the case to court if they so wish.

Building society ombudsman

The building society ombudsman opened his doors for business on July 1, 1987 with power to take decisions on cases which occured after June 1987. The ombudsman reports to a council whose members include consumer champions and society chiefs.

Areas Covered

Problems arising from mortgages and loans, individual share and deposit accounts, foreign exchange transactions and agency payments.

Main Exclusions

Problems about accounts opened by companies and problems about the Financial Services Act. Also the ombudsman cannot look at a complaint until it has been thoroughly investigated by the society's own internal complaints procedure.

Powers

The ombudsman can order compensation of up to £100,000 to be paid. His decision is not binding on the claimant and can only be ignored by the society if they give publicity to the fact that they are not going to comply with the ombudsman's findings. In practice this is likely to mean they will put a note in their report and accounts saying that in such and such a case they disregarded the ombudsman's advice.

Health service ombudsman

This was set up in 1973 and can investigate complaints about actions taken by staff of the health authorities working in the National Health Service. Complaints must be made in writing, initially to the health authority itself and then to the ombudsman.

Areas covered

The most common complaints are about delays in admission, loss of patient's property, lack of information to patients and relatives, inadequate consultation and wrongful detention in psychiatric hospitals.

Main exclusions

Problems in connection with the diagnosis of illnesses, or the care and treatment of a patient, actions of doctors about the services they provide under contract with family practitioner committees, personnel matters like staff pay and complaints made more than one year after the event. Also, he cannot touch complaints about the clinical judgements of doctors, nurses and dental staff, nor look at complaints that could be taken to court.

Powers

The ombudsman can order a government body or health authority to pay compensation or make amends, but they are not bound by the judgement. In practice the vast majority do abide by his findings.

Insurance ombudsman

In 1981 three insurance companies decided to set up an ombudsman. Now over seventy-seven insurance groups taking in 188 member companies are members.

Areas covered

If you are unhappy about the way your claim has been treated, for example, it was not met, was inadequate or delayed, then you can try taking your case to the ombudsman. You must write or telephone him within six months of the date the company rejected your complaint.

Main exclusions

Only complaints about member insurance companies can be looked at. Claims about poor investment performance, actuarial problems, surrender values, bonuses and paid up policy provisions are specifically excluded.

Powers

He can order the insurance company to pay compensation

of up to £100,000. The decision is binding on the company, but you are free to disregard the findings and go to court if you wish.

Local ombudsman

There are five local ombudsmen in Britain, and they have been working since 1974. They cover

- Greater London, the South East and East Anglia
- North of England, North Midlands
- Scotland
- Wales

They investigate complaints about local authorities, joint planning boards, water authorities and police authorities.

Areas covered

Neglect and unjustified delay, malice or unfair discrimination, faulty ways of doing things, failure to tell people their rights.

Main exclusions

They cannot question a council's decision. There must be a complaint that something specific went wrong. This excludes complaints about events which affect all or most of the local inhabitants, like the rates going up or personnel matters. Nor can they deal with complaints about a police officer. An independent organisation called the Police Complaints Authority will investigate serious complaints about police and will doublecheck the results of investigations into less serious complaints. In the first instance write down clearly what happened if you are making a complaint about the police and send it to police officer's chief constable.

Power

The ombudsman can order compensation payments or ask for matters to be put right. However, his findings are not binding on the local authority. He cannot investigate any complaint which could be taken to court or appeal.

Parliamentary ombudsman

This position was established in 1967 to look into complaints from the public about the way they have been treated by government departments.

Areas covered

To investigate matters where someone claims to have sustained injustice as a consequence of maladministration by a civil servant. The ombudsman looks at the way government departments deal with the public.

Main exclusions

Complaints about government policy or legislation, crime, personnel matters like pay and actions or decisions taken by independent statutory authorities. He cannot look at any complaint that could be taken to court.

Powers

He can order the government department to pay compensation or make amends, but his decision is not binding on either party. In practice, with the weight of parliament behind him, he is virtually guaranteed 100% success.

Personal insurance arbitration service

A more recent innovation. This service was set up in 1981 by several insurance companies who did not wish to join the insurance ombudsman scheme. It now has sixty-five member companies. Disputes are settled by an arbitrator from the Chartered Institute of Arbitrators. If you opt for arbitration both parties are bound by the decision and you forfeit your rights under the law.

Areas covered

Complaints from people who claim to have suffered financial loss through alleged failure of the insurance company to fulfil its obligations under a specific insurance contract.

Main exclusions

Complaints about non-member companies and about disputes which arise from third parties or insurance taken out by employers. Both parties must agree to arbitration before the arbitrator can proceed with the case. The arbitrator can only take on claims when the normal complaints procedure of the insurance company has been exhausted.

Powers

The arbitrator can award compensation of between £25,000 and £100,000, although each life assurance company is free to set its own limits within this range. The arbitrator's findings are binding on both parties. The insurance company is responsible for all costs of the arbitration except for any of the costs involved in the customer preparing and submitting documents and/or attending a hearing which is at the arbitrator's discretion.

Office of the industrial insurance commissioner

The granddaddy of them all, set up by the Industrial Assurance Act of 1923, its members are all the life assurance companies selling industrial life assurance, which is defined as policies where premiums are collected weekly or monthly in person by the salesman. The biggest names are the Prudential, the Pearl, the Refuge and London and Manchester. The commissioner, who has a legal background, acts as the arbitrator. The hearings are informal and the customer does not have to turn up at court.

Areas covered

Disputes about claims, amounts paid out, delays in payment on industrial life assurance contracts. People with complaints should first ask the company concerned to look at the matter, then if that does not work, you can write to the industrial life commissioner putting all the facts clearly and enclosing copies of any relevant correspondence.

Powers

The findings of the arbitrator are legally binding on the company and there is no limit to the level of compensation. When compensation is awarded a small charge is due. For a typical £300 award, the policyholder would have to pay a fee of £23.50. The minimum fee is £4 with a top limit of £42.

Solicitors complaints bureau

This was set up on September 1, 1986 to investigate complaints about solicitors. Previously the Law Society had dealt with these, but there had been such a massive increase in complaints that under the old system there were long delays before these could be resolved. The investigation committee is made up of seven lay members and four solicitors.

Areas covered

If you think the solicitor's work is not up to scratch, you can make a complaint under the 'shoddy work' provision. Most frequent complaints are about delays in completing work or failure to keep in touch.

Main exclusions

Anything relating to charges on commercial work.

Powers

If the bureau decides your solicitor has been negligent, they will put you in touch with a panel of solicitors who will advise whether you have a legal case. If it is decided the solicitor is guilty of serious misconduct, the independent solicitors' disciplinary tribunal can fine, reprimand, suspend or strike off the solicitor involved. However they cannot order the solicitor to pay compensation.

Investment

There are expected to be five self-regulatory organisations when the full brunt of the Financial Services Act becomes law. In addition, members of what will be called recognised professional bodies e.g. solicitors, accountants, will have to provide customers with an equivalent source of independent investigation as these organisations in order to be 'recognised' under the act i.e. in order for their members to be able to give investment advice legally.

The Securities and Investment Board is discussing the details of various schemes proposed by the self-regulatory organisations and recognised professional bodies, the former are proposing informal investigation procedures while the latter seem to favour arbitration schemes.

As well as independent investigation procedures with powers of varying degrees to enforce monetary settlements, everyone who buys an investment from an authorised person can seek compensation from a central body, called the

Financial Services Compensation Manager Ltd, if the firm they deal with goes bust. Investors will receive 100% of the first £30,000 and 90% of the next £20,000. Recognised professional bodies will have to provide an equivalent scheme. Insurance companies and building societies will be exempt because their products are already covered by statutory compensation schemes. Insurance policies will remain covered by the Policyholders Protection Act which gives consumers up to 90% protection with no ceiling, while those dealing with building societies will be slightly worse off as they are covered for 90% of the first £20,000 only. People dealing with banks are at the bottom of the list. They are covered for 75% of the first £20,000 only.

OMBUDSMAN	No. of Enquiries	No. of cases investigated	Decisions
Banking Ombudsman	2747	1748	345 complaints rejected 26 complaints settled 407 complaints file open
Building Society Ombudsman	no information available		
Health Service Ombudsman	1048	483	290 justified
Insurance Ombudsman	5873	1240	785 company decision confirmed 218 company decisions revised 14 case withdrawn
Local Ombudsman	3502	310 516*	232 maladministration 78 no maladministration
Office of the Industrial Assurance Com.	no information published		
Parliamentary Ombudsman	914	168	88 fully justified 80 partly justified 23 not justified
PIAS	no information published		
Solicitors Complaint bureau	no information published		

CHAPTER SIX: SHOPPING SMART

You probably do not realise it but during the course of every day you are likely to enter into several contracts. When you buy your train ticket, your lunch or the daily paper you make a simple contract. The same applies when you go out shopping. As a consumer you should be aware that these contracts are protected by The Sale of Goods Act (1979) and The Consumer Protection Act (1987).

A simple contract is no more than one person making an offer and the other person accepting it. It can be verbal or in writing. Strangely enough, when a shopkeeper displays his or her goods, this is not an offer. He or she is inviting the public to make an offer for them – legally called an 'invitation to treat'. The contract is made when the retailer accepts your offer. This means that if there is a mistake on the price ticket you have no right to insist that the goods are sold at that figure or indeed, sold at all.

As a buyer, you have some very important rights each and every time you make a purchase. They are that the goods:

- *Correspond to their description*

The seller will be in breach of the contract if this is not the case. E.g., if you buy a shirt, labelled size 15 and when you get home, you find it is too small, as it is actually size 14.

- *Are of merchantable quality*

This simply means the goods are not broken or damaged.

- *Are fit for their purpose*

Goods must be able to perform their normal function, e.g., scissors must cut and glue must stick. In addition, if you buy an item for a specific purpose, known to the seller, and on the strength of his or her recommendation, then these goods must meet your stated requirements.

When things go wrong

If the goods don't come up to scratch, you can take several courses of action:

1. You can return the item and have a cash refund for the full amount paid. If appropriate, you can also sue for damages.
2. If the shopkeeper offers a price reduction, you can still press for a full refund if you wish, or you may choose to accept.
3. You can agree to a repair at the shopkeeper's expense.
4. You can accept a credit note, but make sure it is dated and valid for a reasonable period of time.

Remember:

- You have the same rights whether you have paid in cash or by credit. If you have used your credit card and cannot gain satisfaction from the retailer, then try the credit card company itself.
- You have a contract with the retailer and it is illegal for them to refuse to repay you by blaming the fault on the manufacturer.
- You don't need a receipt to prove your purchase, but it obviously helps. You can also produce a credit card counter-foil or a friend as a witness if necessary.
- It is difficult to know how long you can expect an article to last before a defect develops. This will obviously depend on the specific goods bought and you should take this into account when complaining.
- If you change your mind when you get home and want to swop the goods, you have no legal rights.
- Your rights cannot be taken away by any exclusion clause included in the agreement by the trader or displayed in the store. Signs saying 'no money back' or 'no exchanges' are not valid and do not affect your statutory rights.
- You lose your rights if a defect is pointed out to you before you buy and you still go ahead with the purchase. The same applies if you buy a defective item after careful examination and the flaw was easily noticeable.

Goods that come with a guarantee give you extra rights under The Sale of Goods Act (1979). Any limitations, such as time or parts, put in the guarantee are not valid if they are an attempt to deprive you of your statutory rights. Guarantees can be a good second line of defence if you have problems with the trader. In many cases, guarantees are offered for such a reasonable length of time that they extend your protection under The Sale of Goods Act. Also, they have a positive advantage in that the benefits of the guarantee are transferable to a third party. For example, if the goods are given to a third party they are still covered by the guarantee whereas under The Sale of Goods Act the protection only extends to the purchaser.

Second hand goods

You have the same rights under The Sale of Goods Act as you do with new goods. However, merchantable quality and fitness of purpose will very much depend on the age of the goods and the price you pay.

Private sales

You have no general rights under The Sale of Goods Act if you buy from a private individual, e.g. you answer a small advertisement in the local paper. However, you do have the right to insist that the goods correspond with their description, otherwise you can sue the seller for your money back. Unfortunately, this is often easier said than done. Sometimes the seller has flown the nest and frequently the costs involved in seeking redress outweigh any advantages.

Stolen goods

A seller must own the goods or at least have a right to dispose of them. If the goods do not belong to the seller in the first place, they cannot legally become your property even after you have paid for them. This can cause a problem in the most innocent of circumstances. Both buyer and seller can genuinely believe the sale is valid. However, goods may have been stolen and passed to the present owner without his or her knowledge of the theft. If the real owner can trace and prove ownership, he or she can recover the property without having to repay the current owner. If you are caught in this type of chain all you can do is to try to reclaim your money from the person who sold you the goods. There is one major exception to this rule. Goods bought at a bona fide market, that is one established by law, become the legal property of the buyer and cannot be recovered even if it can be proved subsequently that they have been lost or stolen. This is an ancient piece of legislation called 'market overt' and applies to markets such as London's Portobello Road and Petticoat Lane.

Auctions

At an auction you basically forfeit your rights under The Sale of Goods Act. You certainly have no protection as far as merchantable quality goes. However, you have some limited cover under the Misrepresentation Act (1967) if the article proves to be a fraud, i.e. if you buy a Victorian desk which turns out to be a reproduction. There are certain regulations covering auctions:

1. Sales are binding only when the auctioneer brings the hammer down. Until that moment the bidder can withdraw his or her bid and the auctioneer can withdraw the article from the sale.
2. A reserve price can be set. The auctioneer will obviously know what it is, but bidders need not be told. If the highest bid is below the reserve price, the article need not be sold at that price.
3. A seller can bid for his own goods at an auction. However, he or she must give notice to the other bidders of this. If a seller does bid without informing the auction, any subsequent sales that are made, are not legally binding. The buyers are entitled to return the goods and have a full refund.
4. An auctioneer can buy articles but only with the seller's permission. If this permission is granted then no commission can be charged on such sales. Anyone can claim against an auctioneer if they think he or she has cheated by buying on their own account and without the seller's permission.
5. It is illegal for two or more dealers to get together and form a 'dealing ring'. A 'ring' exists when the dealers agree only one of their number will bid. This eliminates

competitive bidding and may keep the price from rising to the level it might otherwise have reached.
6. Auctioneers must not pretend to accept bids, called 'taking them out of the air'.

Sales

There used to be a time when a sale was something of a special event. Most stores only held them once or twice a year and you were often able to find a genuine bargain. Nowadays they are so frequent you may well wonder if you are really saving any money.

Goods bought at bargain or reduced prices are still covered by The Sale of Goods Act and you lose none of your legal rights. They must correspond with the description and be of merchantable quality, unless clearly marked otherwise by labels such as 'shopsoiled' or 'seconds'.

Price reductions can be a problem area:

1. Where a previous price is shown, for example, reduced from £10 to £5, the item must have been on display in that shop or another named branch for at least twenty-eight consecutive days in the last six months at the higher price. In addition, there must have been at least one purchase at the higher price. Unfortunately, it is quite legal for a shop to print a disclaimer for this twenty-eight day period, provided they clearly point out that these conditions have not been met. This often happens when a store buys in 'special purchases' for a sale.
2. It is illegal to make a comparison with the alleged worth of the goods. For example, a sign saying 'worth £20, price here only £10' is not allowed.
3. If a price comparison is made with a recommended retail price, it must be a price applicable to that locality. Shops are not allowed to make vague allusions to prices elsewhere.

A new act called The Consumer Protection Act, became law in 1987. So far Part 1 and Part 2 have come into effect – and these cover product liability and general safety requirements. Part 3 comes into effect on a date to be announced and will cover the following:

- To make it an offence to give any misleading indication

to consumers about the price of goods, services, accommodation or facilities.

- To set up a voluntary code of practice to give traders guidance on how to avoid making misleading statements.

If you think you have been misled by a sign displayed at a sale, your best course of action is to report it to the local trading standards officer at your local town hall.

Price aside, your rights are exactly the same as at any other time. Goods do not have to be exchanged unless they are faulty. Some shops who usually offer to exchange perfect goods often withdraw this concession during sale time which is within their rights.

What happens if you purchase an article in the sale and you were charged the normal price? If the item was marked 'non sale' you have no come-back. However, if it was not the shop may have committed a criminal offence under the Trade Descriptions Act. Consider reporting them to the trading standards officer at your local council who might decide to take legal action against the retailer. Unfortunately, you are unlikely to get a refund of the extra cash you paid out, even if the council does decide to prosecute. Although you have the right to ask the court to order a refund, there is no guarantee it will do so.

Mail order

You have the same legal rights when buying by mail order as you do when buying from a shop. Adverts and catalogues inviting people to shop by post must show the supplier's name and business address, a post office box number is not allowed. No contract exists until the supplier accepts an order. However, once the goods or an acknowledgement of the order is sent then a binding contract exists.

Various codes of practice have been drawn up to protect people buying by mail order. These codes lay down guidelines which member companies must stick to, otherwise they can be expelled. Most codes also build in compensation schemes if things go wrong. The principal organisations are:

1. Mail Order Traders Association (MOTA). Many of the glossy catalogues belong to this association.

2. Association of Mail Order Publishers (AMOP) – for book and record publishers.
3. Newspaper Publishers Association (NPA) – this covers all the national daily and Sunday newspapers.
4. Newspaper Society – this covers regional and local papers.
5. Periodical Publishers Association – covers many magazines.
6. National Newspaper Mail Order Protection Scheme (MOPS). This covers advertisements in national newspapers. It relates to specifically described products but not services or goods bought from catalogues.

As well as these, the Advertising Standards Authority (ASA) administer a code of practice which should be followed by publishers and advertising agencies. The main rules are:

- Suppliers should provide an inspection sample of their goods at the address shown on the advertisement.
- Refund of payment available in full if goods are returned undamaged within seven days of receipt. You do not have to give a reason for their return.
- Goods should be sent to you within twenty-eight days of receipt of order, otherwise a full refund should be given.

  There are certain exceptions to this, such as 'made to measure' articles.

Unsolicited goods

Sometimes called inertia selling. This practice seems to be less common now that people are wise to it, e.g. if an unsolicited parcel of goods was dropped through your letterbox, you should:

1. Do nothing. If the firm does not collect the item in six months then it is legally yours. The sender can have the goods back during this period, if they come to collect them or send you the postage to return them.
2. Write a letter, saying they should be collected from your address. If the goods are not collected within thirty days, they are yours to keep.
3. Above all, ignore any threats or demands for payment. They are strictly illegal.

Delivery appointments

Why is it that shops are always so vague about fixing a firm delivery date? It is frustrating when you stay in and wait and wait and wait . . . Unfortunately, there is very little you can do about it, other than insist that the goods are delivered as soon as possible.

One way you can give yourself some rights is to insist on an exact date and time for delivery, and make this part of the contract. You should preferably put the date in writing on the order form. This is called 'making time of the essence'. If the date or time is broken, you have the right to cancel the contract and claim back anything you have paid.

If goods are delivered which are faulty, you can insist the seller collects them. When you sign for the goods always write 'Received but not checked' and delete any reference to the goods being delivered in perfect condition. You must tell the seller immediately that you are rejecting the item.

Deposits

A deposit is normally a token of good faith. It shows the retailer or seller you are serious about wanting to buy the item or service. Your rights depend on the circumstances:

1. In England and Wales, a deposit on a house purchase is refundable up to the date you exchange contracts. After that you are legally bound to complete the purchase and if you fail to do so, you lose the deposit.
2. If you ask for a special article which has to be ordered you will usually be asked for a deposit. If you don't complete the purchase your money is not refundable.
3. If you ask for goods to be put aside you may have to pay a deposit. If you decide not to buy the goods you should be able to get your money back, provided you stick to the defined time limit. Most shops will set goods aside for a few hours at no charge.
4. You will be asked for a deposit when you hire goods, e.g. glasses from an off-licence. Your deposit will be returned in full when the glasses are returned but the shopkeeper can deduct costs for any breakages.

Presents

Suppose you give a present which turns out to be defective. Your friend takes it back to the shop where it was bought. The shopkeeper refuses to exchange it. Is the shop within law? Strictly speaking, the answer is 'yes'. The contract is not with your friend but with you, the purchaser. Your friend has no legal relationship with the shop and therefore no legal remedy.

One way around this archaic system would be to include the transfer of your legal rights at the same time as the gift was presented, e.g. 'To Fred with all my love and my rights under The Sale of Goods Act, 1979'. However, you would have to give the shop notice in writing of the gift and the transfer of your rights. And you only thought the law was an ass!

Quotations

A quotation is a firm price for which the trader will do a job. If there will be VAT on top, then this should be made clear, otherwise you can assume the price includes VAT. An estimate is an indication of a final price, but you must allow for a variation. This has to be reasonable, but as they say in the building trade 'how long is a piece of string'. Estimates can cause all sorts of problems and a firm quote is normally the best solution. You do not have to pay a fee for a quote unless you have agreed one in advance.

Going bust

If you buy goods from a shop which subsequently goes bust, getting a refund on faulty goods is likely to be almost impossible. If the business is a limited company, your only option is to sue the company, but you will be low down on the list of priorities for the liquidator. If the business was a partnership or sole trader, you can take action against any partner in the firm.

Office of Fair Trading

The Office of Fair Trading is the consumer's watchdog. Although it comes under the control of the Department of Trade and Industry, it is in fact independent of the government. It is headed by a director-general who is neither a politician nor a civil servant. It does not handle individual complaints but keeps an overall watch on the market place.

Its main areas of responsibility are:

1. Codes of practice
   It issues guidelines on trading conduct for a wide range of industries.
2. New laws
   It makes recommendations about changes to existing consumer laws and advises about bringing in new laws.
3. Restrictive trade practices
   It will take action, if the consumer is placed at a potential disadvantage.
4. Action against traders
   It will monitor and prosecute traders who break consumer law.
5. Consumer Credit Act
   It is responsible for the licensing of providers of credit.
6. Monopolies
   The director-general makes recommendations to the Monopolies Commission on the need for further investigation if he thinks a merger would be against the public interest.

CHAPTER SEVEN: CREDITABLE TREATMENT

Credit has existed ever since mankind first learned the art of trading. In the beginning people pledged the fruits of their next harvest in return for food they needed straight away. When barter was replaced by buying goods for cash, credit transactions became more complex. The moneylenders and pawnbrokers of yesteryear have turned into the high street banks and finance houses of today.

Our whole monetary system is now built on a credit pyramid. The pound in your pocket is not backed by any specific tangible wealth as it used to be when sterling was linked to the gold standard. Instead its purchasing power reflects nothing more or less than sentiment. The value of the pound mirrors Britain's international financial standing.

Just as many countries around the world live on credit, including the USA and a large part of the so-called Third World, so do an increasing number of British families. The level of debt has grown dramatically in this country over the past twenty years as statistics from the Bank of England show. At the end of 1987, the banks were lending £50 billion to personal customers compared to £40 billion a year earlier. Britain's consumers owe a total of £200 billion if all lending by building societies, banks, credit card companies, finance companies and retailers is added together compared to around £100 billion five years ago, according to the Central Statistical Office.

Consumer Credit Act

During 1971 and 1972 the Crowther Committee established by the Wilson government delivered its report on the issues raised by this boom in credit. It came to the conclusion that customers needed greater protection against loan sharks, misleading advertisements on the cost of loans and strictly defined rights of redress. The culmination of the committee's work was the introduction in July 1974 of the Consumer Credit Act. However, it was not till more than a decade later in May 1985 that the bulk of its recommendations became law. Since then there have been piecemeal additions but the Act itself forms the cornerstone of consumers' rights in the increasingly cut throat area of credit.

The Consumer Credit Act regulates the form and content of credit agreements. In broad terms it covers loans to individuals of less than £15,000 and hire purchase agreements of more than three months duration. Under the act agreements are basically divided into three categories:

- land agreements
- non-cancellable agreements
- cancellable agreements

Most people will probably not come across land agreements. They are, as their name implies, credit agreements where you are putting up land or property, such as your home, as security. In this case the rules are designed to give you plenty of time to study the agreement in your own home without being hassled by the would-be lender. You must be given seven days to study the agreement without being badgered by the finance company. After this time you will be sent a signed and dated offer of credit, together with a copy of the original agreement and any related mortgage documents. You then have a further seven days to think about the deal. Once you have signed and returned the offer document, you are committed and cannot change your mind. Up till that stage you can back down without any penalty.

Consumers have least protection when they sign credit agreements on business premises, say in a shop or bank. In this case, the moment you sign you are committed. There is no cooling off period. However, if a second signature is required from someone who is not present then the agreement no longer becomes one which is arranged on business premises and therefore it turns into a cancellable document.

As their name implies, cancellable agreements are just that – you can change your mind and you are not committed to taking the credit or paying a penny. However, these type of agreements are only available in certain strictly defined circumstances, when the forms are not signed on office premises and when you were persuaded to take out the loan after a sales pitch.

If both these two conditions apply then you have a five-day cooling off period in which you can change your mind and cancel the agreement. This cooling off period starts from the day after you receive your copy of the agreement. If you do change your mind make sure you send your cancellation by registered post by the end of the fifth day. If you post it later than this then your cancellation will not be valid and you will have to take the credit.

If the agreement was signed at home but you were not subject to any sales pitch then it cannot be cancelled. Watch out for telephone sales calls. Strictly speaking these salespeople are technically in their offices, so it does not count as selling in your home and such agreement cannot be cancelled.

There is one exception to the above rules. Under the act contracts which can be cancelled have to include specially printed notices explaining how, when and where to cancel. Without this information it is not a legally binding document. To save costs many firms only print and use cancellable agreement forms. If you sign one of these then you have the right to cancel, even if the document was signed on the business premises.

What happens when you cancel? Basically, it is as if you never signed. You do not have to pay the company a penny and, of course, must return any goods you cannot afford. They in turn must send back to you any goods you had given as part payment or security for the loan.

Loans not covered by the Consumer Credit Act 1974 include:

- Borrowing by limited companies.
- Building society mortgages.
- Small trade credits, such as the weekly paper bill or the monthly account at the corner shop.
- Accounts which have to be totally cleared each month. Your monthly bills from American Express and Diners Club come within this category.

- Loan agreements where there are less than five repayments.
- Bank overdrafts under £15,000 are regulated but do not have to have written agreements.

Apart from the critical distinction between agreements which are immediately binding and those which can be cancelled, there is another important distinction to keep in mind. This is the difference between so-called 'debtor-creditor-supplier' agreements, where the money is lent for a specific transaction, e.g. to buy a TV, and so-called 'debtor-creditor' agreements where a cash loan is made which is not tied to any particular purchase.

The difference between the two is very important, although not always apparent at first glance. If you borrow funds under a 'debtor-creditor-supplier' agreement, sometimes referred to as a purchaser agreement, then the company lending you the money can be held responsible for any defects in the goods on an equal basis with the shop supplying the goods. This means if the shop goes bust or refuses to refund your money you have a second bite of the cherry. Credit cards issued after July 1, 1977 when used to buy goods give you this added protection. However, if you simply borrowed money from a bank or used your credit card to withdraw cash from an automated teller machine and subsequently spent the funds on a purchase, you would not be covered.

Remember before you put pen to paper to sign a loan agreement you are entitled to full written details about the charges, repayments etc. Read this carefully and at your leisure before making a final decision.

When you sign a credit agreement you end up with lots of bits of paper. If you sign the agreement on the premises of the store or financial company then you will be given a spare copy to keep. If you are sent an agreement to sign, then a duplicate must be enclosed for your files. What is more, the company must send you a copy of your signed copy within seven days of you returning it to them.

You can also insist on receiving copies of any mortgage documents you sign. If you guarantee a loan then you have the legal right to copies of any forms signed in connection with the transaction. Do not despair if you lose your copy of the contract, you have the right to receive a duplicate. You must put your request in writing and may be asked to pay a small fee, usually around 50p.

True cost

One of the most important aspects of the Consumer Credit Act is that for the first time it established the consumer's right to know the true cost of credit in most circumstances. Interest and credit charges must be disclosed and the true annual percentage rate, known as APR, must be clearly shown. This APR must be calculated according to an agreed formula and has to take into account all the charges involved in setting up the loan. For example, it must include any arrangement fee.

It is quite common for companies to quote flat rates of interest on loans which are very misleading as they do not take into account the pattern of repayments and reduced size of the loan over the period of the agreement. For instance, suppose you borrow £100 at a flat rate of 10% and this must be repaid quarterly in four equal instalments. In reality you are borrowing £100 for three months, £75 for six months, £50 for nine months and £25 for twelve months, but the rate assumes you are borrowing the whole £100 for the full year. By taking into account the repayments the 10% flat rate of interest balloons into a 16% true rate.

There are two common traps to watch out for. First, there is a loophole under the Consumer Credit Act which permits brokers and companies who are arranging loans for you not to add their administration charges to the quoted APR from the lender itself. Second, keep an eye out for companies who insist loans are repaid by insurance policies. They often advertise heavily in the national press. Most loans are repaid early and the policy is surrendered. Since you do not get all your money back if you surrender an insurance policy in the first few years there is a hidden cost to these loans.

Canvassing

Unless you specifically requested in writing a visit from a salesman offering credit only licensed salespeople can call without you asking them and then sell you something on credit. It is also an offence to send anyone under the age of eighteen any document inviting them to either apply for credit or buy goods on credit.

Repayments

Under the law, the lender must send you a detailed statement of what you owe, what you have paid and when the balance is due. You have the right at any time to ask how much is required to repay the loan and, providing you give due notice, to settle your debt in full. With a bank loan this is usually relatively straightforward, but life can become a bit more complex with hire purchase agreements, where much depends on the small print.

On the other hand if, far from wanting to pay off the loan early, you fall into arrears, then the company must give you notice before taking steps to reclaim the goods or secure the cash. The lender must serve a default notice on you giving you seven days to put the matter right.

If you think you are paying too high a rate of interest then you have the legal right to ask a county court to change the terms of the agreement. The onus will fall on the lender to show that the terms are reasonable. Similarly the courts can make null and void agreements which 'grossly contravene the ordinary principles of fair dealings'. They can also scrap any parts of the contract which they regard as too penal.

Providers of credit

The Consumer Credit Act also regulates those people and companies who are permitted to offer credit. Under the act anyone who offers credit must be licensed by the Office of Fair Trading. In 1987 197,733 companies held such licences. They included banks, hire purchase companies, finance houses, shops, rental firms, debt collectors, debt adjusters, credit reference agencies, and financial advisers. To obtain a licence companies need to get an application form from the Office of Fair Trading called 'Application and information in support of a standard licence'. The licence cost varies from £80 for sole traders carrying out limited loan business to £210 for larger firms.

The aim of the licensing system is to curb unfair practices. Companies can lose their licence if they contravene the rules laid down by the Consumer Credit Act – for example, cold calling on loans is strictly forbidden. It is a criminal offence for an unlicensed person to offer loans and any agreements they do enter into cannot subsequently be enforced without the specific consent of the Office of Fair Trading.

Refusal of credit

No one likes being refused a loan. While there is nothing you can do to force a company to lend you money, you can make sure their decision was not based at least in part on faulty information. You can, for example, ask if the company used a credit reference agency. If they did, you can check for a small fee that the information about you on the agency's files is accurate.

The best known agencies are The United Association for the Protection of Trade, known as UAPT – Infolink Plc, and CCN. They accumulate lists of people who have defaulted on hire purchase and credit agreements in the past. In addition, they search the Registry of County Court Judgements to find out the names of people with debts still outstanding. In this way, they build up a black list of people who may be considered poor credit risks.

If you think you have been refused credit because of a credit reference agency report, here's what to do:

1. Request in writing from the trader concerned the name and address of any agency that has been consulted for information on you. You must do this within twenty-eight days of the refusal. The trader, in turn, has seven days to give you this information, although there is no obligation to send you details of the contents of the report itself.
2. Apply to the agency concerned in writing for a copy of any file they hold on you. You must enclose a fee of £1. It is best to give your full name and any recent addresses.
3. The agency must reply in seven working days. If they have a file on you, this must be enclosed. They must also send you details of how the file can be corrected.
4. If any of the information they hold is incorrect, you may write requesting correction. If they refuse or fail to reply in twenty-eight days then you can write your own correction note.
5. The agency may wish to doublecheck your statement. If

this is accurate, they should inform you in writing when the correction has been made.

6. They must use the corrected report in the future. In addition, they must send it to anyone who has consulted them about you in the preceding six months.

If you have any problems obtaining a report or having a report corrected, then you should consult the director general of the Office of Fair Trading. Send full details together with copies of all previous correspondence with the agency and the lender you approached.

Debt collectors

Debt collectors require licences from the director general of the Office of Fair Trading. It is a criminal offence to operate in this area without one. There are statutory limitations on the way debt collectors can run their business:

- They cannot harass a debtor by making threatening or frequent demands for payment.
- They cannot make regular threats to sue.
- They cannot make demands accompanied by undue publicity, e.g. taking out an advertising hording.
- Their offices or shops cannot publish a public list of bad debts, sometimes called a 'shame list'.
- Trade organisations can exchange lists of debtors privately, although this must not be with the intention of forcing someone to pay.

Types of credit

There are a growing number of providers of credit, including stores such as Marks and Spencer, John Lewis and Harrods, as well as financial companies. The most popular types of credit are:

- Bank Loans and Overdrafts
- Credit Cards
- Charge Cards and Budget Accounts
- Hire Purchase
- Finance House Loans
- Mail Order

Bank loans and overdrafts

Most banks encourage their customers to take out a personal loan when they want to borrow money. A higher rate of interest is charged on these loans than on overdrafts so they are more profitable. You do not have the right to insist on an overdraft or ordinary loan, rather than a personal loan. So if you are not happy about paying the cost of a personal loan, then your only option is to vote with your feet and knock on another bank's door. Personal loan rates are fixed at the outset for the period of the loan. So even if interest rates go down your loan is locked into the old rate. Of course, this works to your advantage if rates go up. While you normally have to state what you need the money for, you are under no obligation to use the money for this purpose.

If the bank is keen to keep your business, it might agree to giving you an ordinary loan. Here, the interest rate is fixed at so many points about base rate and will fluctuate in line with interest rates in the economy as a whole.

Unlike a personal loan, an overdraft is only partially protected by the Customer Credit Act. It is called a 'running account' credit and is treated in much the same way as a store budget account. The key points to remember are:

- Amounts over £15,000 and company borrowings are not covered by the Consumer Credit Act.
- You do not need to have a formal written agreement. Word of mouth will do or a letter confirming the arrangement.
- Overdrafts are theoretically repayable on demand, although this is rarely put to the test. However, if you exceed your limit without permission the bank can refuse to pay your cheques and suspend the overdraft without notice. Your bank manager should give you some form of warning before this happens.
- If the bank agrees a limit, but you do not keep to the agreed figure, it can sue you for its money. However, it must first issue an enforcement notice. This gives you seven days grace to put matters right.
- It is quite common in this country for people to overdraw their account without permission. If the bank thinks you

are creditworthy it will pay the cheque. At the same time you will be charged a much higher than normal interest rate. The bank has no obligation to pay your cheque if you do not have the money in your account. If it allows an 'unauthorised' overdraft, it can demand the money back at any time without an enforcement notice.

The overdraft has traditionally been one of the cheapest ways of borrowing money. But no more – particularly for personal customers. The banks have changed the rules recently and introduced what they call a 'managed' rate of interest on overdrafts. This is a fixed rate which you pay on a monthly basis when your account dips into the red – and it is a lot more expensive than the informal overdraft arrangement of old.

- Beware of arrangement fees if you ask for an overdraft. Banks seem to charge them without so much as a bye your leave. They can often be as much as 1% of the amount you borrow. These extra fees are hard to justify – so if your bank does try to charge you one, make sure you make a big fuss about it. Most banks will withdraw them if you protest hard enough, especially if they do not want to lose your business.

Credit cards

In days of old, a man's status and wealth could be assessed by the number of cattle he owned – or perhaps the number of wives! Now it is the number of credit cards he has stacked in his wallet. Although not with us yet, the days of the cashless society draw nearer. Plastic will soon be all powerful.

Each type of card gives a different financial service and a different set of rights. However, the one common factor is to encourage you to spend now, pay later – as one advertisement puts it 'take the waiting out of wanting'.

Bank credit cards

Access and Visa cards are issued free by the high street banks. You will be given a fixed credit limit which must not be exceeded. You are sent monthly statements showing your purchases and payment is due twenty-five days later. You can either settle your account in full or repay most of the debt at your own pace over the next few months. A minimum payment of 5% of what you owe, or £5 if under £100, is required within the initial twenty-five day period. If you time it right, you can get seven or eight weeks free credit on purchases made in the UK and even longer on some foreign transactions. Cash advances are available on both cards. Interest is charged monthly on amounts not repaid. Working out the exact interest rate you will pay is always difficult as it depends on the time lag between your purchase and first repayment, as well as how long you take to pay.

Charge cards

American Express and Diners Club are probably the best known, although many people confuse these with credit cards. You pay a joining fee and an annual subscription. Although used in the same way as Access and Visa cards to pay for goods and services they are not credit cards as you must clear your bill in full each month. However, their one big advantage is that there are no fixed spending limits, although the cards are coded so that the retailer knows when to phone for authorisation on large sums.

Gold cards

As the name implies, these cards are designed for high earners or those with large unearned income. American Express was first in the field, followed by the high street banks. From the customer's point of view a gold card is often considered as the ultimate in one-upmanship as it shows you are a person of substantial means. There is no credit limit and you must settle up each month. The annual membership fees are higher than standard charge cards and you must have a certain income level to join, normally between £20,000 and £30,000. However, the cards include an overdraft facility of between £7,500 and £10,000 at very attractive interest rates, normally just 2½% over base rate, but a couple of banks have now introduced a fixed rate, or a minimum rate – so check the fine print carefully. Also, there are generous limits on cheque and cash withdrawals.

Shop and store cards

Virtually all the big store groups, such as Marks and Spencers, House of Fraser, Harrods, now issue their own store card. You'll need to check carefully just what type of card you are being offered. They may be credit cards, operating in the same way as Access or Barclaycard, charge cards where the bill has to be settled in full or even budget accounts, where you agree to save a set sum each month and can borrow up to thirty times your monthly payment. In this last instance, you should check to see whether you earn interest when you are in credit and the true cost of borrowing when you take up the overdraft facility.

Rights under Consumer Credit Act

All credit cards have the full protection of the Consumer Credit Act. However, not all plastic cards are in fact credit cards. For example, charge cards, gold cards, and some store cards do not qualify for protection under this Act as they do not offer credit. The Act regulates your rights and obligations under agreements to supply credit. The credit card company must send you a copy of its credit agreement within seven days of saying it will issue you with a card. When your card is renewed, a further signed copy of your agreement must be sent to you.

For consumers, one particularly valuable protection offered under the Act is that it makes credit card companies equally liable with the supplier if the goods or services you purchased with your credit card do not come up to scratch. This only applies to purchases between £100 and £30,000, even if you only used your card to pay part of the bill, e.g. the deposit on a holiday. In practical terms, if you are making no progress with the supplier – perhaps he has gone bust – this means you have a second line of defence.

The credit card companies officially say that this protection is only offered to cards issued after July 1, 1977, the date on which this part of the Consumer Credit Act came into force. Unofficially, they have agreed voluntarily to extend similar rights to pre-July 1977 holders, but they have imposed an arbitrary limit which will not exceed the amount of credit advanced. In effect, there are two classes of credit card holders, those with pre-1977 and the rest. Suppose you buy a washing machine at a cost of £300 with your credit card and it explodes creating £2,000 worth of damage. The supplier has gone bust and you cannot find anyone to pay up. A card holder who received his or her card after July 1977 can claim against the card company for the full amount, that is £300 plus £2,000, while someone whose card predates July 1977 can only claim for £300. If your card was issued before July 1977 write and ask the company for a new one. Make sure it really is new, i.e. has a different number, not simply a re-issue of your existing card.

Protecting your interests

If a credit card goes astray before you receive it, e.g. it is lost in the post, then you cannot be held liable for any improper use. If a thief buys goods with your card before you have signed it or a receipt for the card, the card company suffers the entire loss.

After you have signed the card, you are bound by the conditions of use which will be sent to you with the card. These conditions theoretically make you responsible for any loss the card company suffers if your card is stolen and used by somebody else. However, under the Consumer Credit Act your maximum liability is £50 when you lose a credit card. You have no liability whatsoever after you have told the company of the loss.

The rules covering most charge cards limit your liability to £50 provided you inform the company as soon as you discover the loss. In practice, it is most unlikely that the card companies will ask you to repay a thief's debts. However, if it is your fault that the card has been misused, e.g. you lent it to a friend, then you will be liable for all the debts run up on it.

The card company can, without warning, stop the use of your card by telling suppliers not to accept it. They publish regular blacklists of customers whose cards have been cancelled which are distributed to retailers. Alternatively they may simply refuse to sanction a specific request from a retailer on the phone. Card companies also stress that they are not liable to the card holder if for any reason the retailer refuses to honour the card. The card company has a contract with the retailer which details the terms on which they will trade with each other. However, the mere display of the credit card company's insignia in the shop window does not give the card holder the legal right to demand the card is accepted.

It is not unknown for computers to make mistakes and you may find you are charged with someone else's purchases. Refuse to pay until the card company has sorted out the problem. Make sure that they refund any interest charged.

Traders who accept credit cards are not allowed to charge you more for the privilege, even though they have to pay the credit card company a small percentage of each transaction. There was a move towards this in the early 1980s, but it is no longer permitted in this country. If a retailer tries to charge you extra for paying with a credit card you should refuse and report the trader to the credit card company. Some retailers offer discounts for cash.

Most credit and charge cards now include free accident insurance if you book your travel with one of the cards. The amount ranges from £20,000 to £250,000.

Paying for goods by phone with your credit card is convenient but raises some difficulties for you, the customer. There is no piece of paper with your signature on it to verify the transaction. However, card companies do check retailers before they are allowed to take telephone orders and if they receive many complaints about a single retailer they will withdraw this facility. The main safeguards are:

- The mail order company should check that the delivery address they have corresponds with the address at the card company.
- If you collect items ordered by phone, such as theatre tickets, you should be asked to show your card and may be asked to sign the saleslip.

Hire Purchase

Current estimates based on Bank of England statistics of our national consumer credit debt run at about £31 billion. Much of this takes the form of Hire Purchase sales. It is very important to undertand the difference between credit sales and Hire Purchase sales. With credit, the goods become your property immediately you pay the deposit and receive them. With Hire Purchase you can take possession of whatever items you have bought but they only become your property once the final instalment has been paid.

Most of the rules on Hire Purchase are now included in the Consumer Credit Act. As the goods are hired rather than purchased, your rights vary from those you have when you buy on credit.

- Agreement.
  The Hire Purchase form must be clearly legible and have a red box printed on it, which indicates that this is a legal agreement.
- Copies.
  You are entitled to receive a copy of the unsigned agreement and a further copy once it has been signed.
- Cooling off period.
  If the contract is signed on business premises, you are legally bound by it and have no right to cancel. However, if you sign it in your own home, you will have a five day cooling off period. During this time you can change your mind and cancel if you want. If you want to opt out, you must post the cancellation by the end of the fifth day.
- Annual Percentage Rate.
  You must be told the true annual rate of interest. A good rule of thumb is that the true annual rate is nearly double a flat rate. This takes into account the monthly repayments you make.
- Cash price.
  The cash price must be clearly set out together with the total purchase price and the amount of each instalment.

So much for your rights, but what about your responsibilities under a Hire Purchase agreement? These are to:

- Keep up your hire payments.
- Take care of the goods.
- Keep the goods insured where the contract says this is required.
- Not sell, pawn, or deal in the goods in any way without the owner's written permission.

Generally speaking if you buy goods covered by a Hire Purchase agreement from the person who has hired them, they do not become your property. However, there is one important exception to this last rule. If you buy a secondhand car and subsequently find it still belongs to a finance company under a Hire Purchase agreement, then you have a legal right to keep it. This concession does not apply to professional motor dealers in the trade. Finance companies keep a central register of Hire Purchase vehicles and can make checks for you.

You have a right at any time to terminate the Hire Purchase contract up to the payment of the last instalment. So if you decide you cannot afford the payments after one year of a three year contract, you can end the agreement. However, this means that the owner takes back second hand goods. To compensate for this, you have to pay an additional sum to bring the total payments up to one half the purchase price. The owner may insist on an extra payment if the goods have not been kept in good condition. The overall effect is that when you have passed the half way stage of a hire purchase agreement, you can return the goods at any time without a financial penalty but before then it may prove expensive.

If you do not keep up the repayments under a Hire Purchase agreement, then the goods may be returned to their legal owner. If you have paid less than one third of what is owed, you must be sent a formal default notice before the goods can be recovered. If you then bring your payments up to date, no further action can be taken against you. Once one third has been paid, the owner has to get a court order before repossessing the goods. Courts can be very sympathetic if financial hardship is involved and may as an alternative order a rescheduling of the payments. Until one third has been paid you are more vulnerable to repossession if payments fall behind.

No one can repossess anything from your own property or land, rented or owned, without a court order. This applies whether or not one third of the purchase price has been paid. Suppose your car is on Hire Purchase and you fall behind with the payments. If it is parked in the road, it can be repossessed after due notice. However, if it is parked in your garage, the Hire Purchase company has to go to court.

If a court order is made against you and the bailiff comes to seize some of your property, they cannot take anything which is currently being bought on Hire Purchase. Legally goods covered by Hire Purchase agreements do not belong to you until the final payment has been made.

Although goods under Hire Purchase agreements are hired, not bought, you are still entitled to the same rights as a cash purchaser under the Supply of Goods Act 1972. If goods are defective in any way, you can return them and claim your money back, or ask for a replacement. You can also sue for damages if necessary, e.g. if your freezer breaks down as a result of a defect and all the food is lost.

Remember that more often than not, your contract is with the finance company and not the shop which sold you the goods. Any claims you wish to make will be against the finance company, which in turn may claim against the shop. The shop in turn may claim against the manufacturer. However, there should be no delay in dealing with your complaints as you need only approach the hire purchase company. Your legal rights cannot be taken away by any exclusion clauses, e.g. any conditions such as 'no exchanges after one month' are unenforceable.

Occasionally a hire purchase company will ask you to supply the name of a guarantor. Normally, this happens if you are under eighteen years of age or if the company is worried about your credit rating. A guarantor is personally liable if you default and can be sued for the money outstanding under the guarantee.

Finance house loan

Finance companies lend money in the same way as the banks – in fact many of them are owned by the high street banks. Very often, these loans are arranged at the point of sale and customers are not always aware of the company they are ultimately dealing with. The loans will then be linked directly to your purchase and the finance house, like the credit card company, is liable for the quality of the goods. Remember:

- Ownership is yours as soon as you take delivery, unlike hire purchase where you have to wait until the final payment.
- You have the same consumer rights as if you had paid cash.

- You must be told the true annual percentage rate on the loan.
- If you are in default, the lender is not allowed to increase the rate of interest.
- If you get behind with your payments, the lender cannot seize the goods you have bought with the loan. However, it is quite likely that the contract gives the lender the right to demand the loan is repaid in full if you are a persistently slow payer.
- You have the right to make early repayment whenever you like. You may be entitled to a full rebate of interest or only a partial rebate, depending on what the contract says.
- You may qualify for tax relief if your purchase of goods or services falls under the Inland Revenue's definition of home improvements provided your mortgage is under the statutory limit, currently £30,000.

Mail order

A convenient way of shopping by post out of a catalogue. You can often spread the payments over a longer period, say 20 weeks or more. There is normally no extra charge if you do this and the cost will be the same as if you were paying in full. Watch out for the price you pay which will often be more expensive in the catalogue than in the high street.

Danger signals

- Watch out for unfair interest rates.

The Consumer Credit Act outlawed penal rates so there should be no excuse for anyone to put themselves in the hands of high charging moneylenders. If you think you are paying too high a rate of interest, you have a legal right to ask a county court to change the terms of the agreement. The onus will fall on the lender to show that the terms are reasonable.

- Keep to the known names.

There are plenty of disreputable firms willing to lend you money – at a price. As a general guideline, keep to the members of the Finance Houses Association.

- Beware of hidden administration charges.

Some credit firms will add these on after they have given you an annual percentage rate and they will turn a cheap looking loan into an expensive one.

- Consolidation loans can be an expensive temptation.

It may look the right thing to put all your debts in one basket and pay off one big loan. However, most of the firms offering this sort of package want a second mortgage on your house and will not hesitate to foreclose if you get behind. The rates of interest will probably be higher than you expect.

- Beware of the insurance add-on.

Some lenders try to insist that you take out an insurance policy to cover to loan. Most loans are repaid early and the policy surrendered. Since you do not get all your money back when you surrender a policy in the first few years, this can amount to an extra hidden cost.

- Always get quotations in writing with interest and charges quoted separately.

Get several offers so that you can compare like with like.

- Find out whether repayments are fixed or go up and down with changing interest rates. Also see if there is any penalty for early repayment.

- Do not over commit yourself.

Above all do not be pressurised into signing something you do not understand. Always take any paperwork away and read it carefully and calmly away from any high pressure salesman.

CHAPTER EIGHT: YOU AND YOUR MORTGAGE

A mortgage is about the longest term credit you can get. These days there are plenty of willing lenders around. Building Societies used to be the traditional source – they lent some £35 billion in 1987. However plenty of other firms are now in on the act including banks of all varieties, insurance companies, local councils and specialist mortgage firms. They all recognise the potential for repeat business and cross selling of other financial and legal services. Mortgage feast has replaced mortgage famine.

With mortgages, the aces are nearly all in the lender's hand. Every lender has a different set of regulations and preferences. Theoretically, they are all in competition with each other. However, as with most financial products, market forces make it difficult for anyone to retain a competitive advantage for very long. In broad terms, the following rules apply.

Borrowing requirement

Three times your annual gross income is the usual sum you can borrow, although there are plenty of variations. If you are buying with someone else, you can also add the second income although usually once only. Alternatively, you can often borrow two and a half times the total of your joint income.

Even if your income and ability to repay qualify you for a mortgage, the amount you borrow must relate to the actual value of the property. Normally the loan will be equivalent to 80% or less of the property's value as assessed by the lender's surveyor. However, a higher percentage may be obtained in certain circumstances, although you will usually be asked to pay a one-off insurance premium to protect the lender against any decline in property values. Most mortgages are for twenty-five years, although some companies insist the loan is repaid by the time you are due to retire while others will extend the loan to thirty years for young borrowers. Some lending institutions run accounts which involve you saving with them for a number of years and in return they guarantee you a mortgage. Read the terms and conditions carefully; usually the guarantee is that they will give your request priority.

Problem properties

There are certain types of property on which you will find it difficult if not impossible to get a mortgage. They are:

- Short leaseholds. The lender will usually insist that the lease is at least twenty years longer than the term of the loan, e.g. if you want a twenty year mortgage, the lease must be at least forty years long.
- Freehold flats. With no landlord to maintain the building, keeping this type of property in good repair is often a problem.
- Certain types of converted flats, for example a badly converted flat which would be difficult to re-sell because of shared access or restrictive covenants in the leasc.
- Unusual properties, such as barns, oasthouses and thatched cottages. These have the added problem of expensive buildings' insurance and, in some cases, you may not even be able to buy cover for certain risks such as fire on a thatched cottage.

Which mortgage

There are broadly three types of mortgages:

- Repayment mortgage

This is the most common type of loan. You repay the loan in monthly instalments which consist of a combination of capital and interest.

There is no obligation for you to buy any life insurance with this type of mortgage. However, it makes sense for borrowers to take out a mortgage protection policy so that in the event of their death the mortgage can be repaid in full and the property will form part of their estate.

- Insurance linked mortgage

During the term of the mortgage you only pay interest on the loan to the lender. The loan itself is repaid from the proceeds of an insurance policy. You therefore have two separate but parallel contracts. There are three main types of insurance linked mortgages:

a. Low-cost endowment
   This consists of two policies, a term policy, which is sufficient to repay the loan in case of death and an endowment policy, which should provide enough capital to repay the mortgage and also, depending on investment conditions and the insurance company's skill, leave you with a tax-free cash sum after you have repaid the mortgage.
b. With-profit endowment
   This is similar to the low-cost endowment but all the cover is provided under endowment policy and not partly by cheaper term assurance. So it is more expensive but the tax-free surplus after the mortgage has been repaid should be much bigger.
c. Unit-linked mortgage
   Your money is invested into a unit-linked fund, which is usually priced on a daily or weekly basis, and it includes full life cover. However, it tends to fluctuate more because the value of your policy depends on the price of your units at the date your policy matures. This contrasts with a traditional endowment policy where you are building up a cash sum slowly and profits made in the early years cannot be taken away from you. However, some unit-linked mortgage policies now guarantee to pay you a certain minimum sum so you know you will have enough funds to clear the mortgage entirely.

   You will not normally be asked to take a medical before buying an endowment mortgage, although some companies, fearful of policyholders suffering from AIDS, now insist two men buying a home together take a blood test.

- Pension linked mortgages

These are not available to everyone. Basically, you repay the mortgage from the proceeds of your pension policy.

As you get tax relief on your pension premiums, the fund can build up tax-free and the lump sum is free of tax this is a very good deal. However, only the self-employed and those in non-pensionable occupations can use their personal pension plans in this way. From January 1988 if the current government's proposals come into force you will be able to opt out of your occupational scheme and choose a personal pension instead although there may be restrictions on the proportion of your pension which you can take as a tax-free lump sum. This will increase the number of people who can buy pension mortgages.

Tax incentive

You can probably see by now that there are few hard and fast rules when it comes to mortgages. There is great scope for flexibility and they can be taken out to suit your individual needs. However, there are two major rights and benefits which every UK taxpayer receives:

- Tax relief on the interest you pay on a mortgage for your main residence up to a maximum of £30,000.
- Any profits you make on the sale of your main residence are tax free.

For most people a mortgage is the only form of borrowing that qualifies for tax relief. This relief is really a government subsidy entitling you to a rebate on the interest you pay on a mortgage on your main residence of up to £30,000. As a basic rate tax payer you receive 25p back for every one pound you pay in interest, while a higher rate tax payer at the 40% band would receive 40p in the pound. In fact, under the system of Mortgage Interest Relief At Source, known as MIRAS, your interest payments are reduced by the appropriate percentage of tax relief. This means you pay the bank, building society or specialist lender the net amount. Until recently this only applied to mortgages under £30,000 so those with larger mortgages had to reclaim the tax relief on the first £30,000 portion via their tax returns. However, from April 6, 1987, all mortgages, no matter what their size, can be included in the MIRAS scheme. This applies both to existing and new loans. For existing loans you will need to get the permission from the inspector of taxes by filling in form MIRAS 84 and for new loans you will need to use form

MIRAS 70. This is worth doing as it is both simpler and cheaper than having to claim the tax relief at the end of the following tax year.

A mortgage document will have to be signed by all the people who own the house. The rules on tax relief will change in August 1988. Until then, unmarried couples who live together or friends who are buying a home together will qualify for £30,000 each. From that date tax relief will be limited to the interest on a £30,000 mortgage regardless of the number of people borrowing to buy the property. This puts married couples who only qualify for one lot of mortgage interest relief on an equal footing with unmarried couples.

Cost

Although mortgages are not regulated under the Consumer Credit Act, lenders at still obliged to quote the true annual percentage rate known as the APR. This will take into account any legal or valuation fees, arrangement fees and whether interest is debited monthly, quarterly or annually. The timing of the interest charge can make a big difference to the true cost of borrowing. Most banks charge interest on the daily balance outstanding, while many building societies charge interest on the outstanding balance at the beginning of each year. You can get a better picture by comparing the monthly repayments on a loan of a certain size from two or more sources.

Strange as it may seem when you take out a mortgage you have no way of knowing how much it will cost you over the years. That's because most mortgages are priced in relation to the cost of money in the economy as a whole. You are entitled to receive a reasonable amount of notice, normally one month, before your interest charges are altered. However, under the terms of your mortgage you agree to pay the new charges whatever they may be.

With an endowment linked mortgage, you have no flexibility as the life policy is designed to pay out a cash sum in a fixed term of years. However, with repayment mortgages, you may be able to renegotiate the term of the mortgage with the lender. This means if an increase in interest rates makes your repayments unmanageable, you can often reduce the payments by spreading them over a longer term.

Insurance policy trap

A mortgage is only a fancy name for a long term loan. It is not that long ago that most mortgages were the straightforward repayment variety, perhaps with some form of protection cover. Suddenly all the lenders realised that there was a lot of money to be made by selling insurance policies at the same time. The reason is quite simple – they get up front commission.

Very often you will only be offered a mortgage as part of a package which involves taking out an insurance policy. There is no legal compulsion for you to accept this. Not everyone needs an insurance policy. You may already have sufficient life cover from another source, say your employer's death in service benefit. In addition you may not be able to afford the extra money the premiums will cost, especially if you are a first time buyer.

If the lender will not compromise and offer you an ordinary repayment loan, you will have to shop around until you can find one. Some lenders, especially the banks, will insist on an insurance linked mortgage and also that you transfer your bank account to them. One or two of them will offer a mix of part repayment and part insurance. This can be quite useful if you are trading up your house and you already have an insurance linked mortgage policy which you do not want to surrender.

Building societies officially work to a code of practice which states that they will not make it a condition of the loan that the borrower takes out an insurance policy or uses some other service. You should be on your guard against getting the impression that the mortgage will be speeded up should you take out an endowment policy. Also make sure you hear all the options, not only insurance linked ones but also repayment mortgages.

Although you may not need any more life cover, it is always wise to take out some form of mortgage protection, especially if you have dependents. That way, if you die, at least the mortgage will be repaid. The premiums will be much cheaper than an endowment policy. The lender will not earn so much commission, but it may be enough to satisfy his honour as a salesman!

Repayment difficulties

If you run into any problem with your repayments, it is essential that you inform the lender straight away. You have entered into a contract to repay the loan and if you do not, the lender has the right to foreclose and sell the property. This is very much a last resort. Banks and building societies bend over backwards to be helpful. There are various ways in which a temporary cash crisis can be resolved:

- Interest-only payments for a few months. This only applies to repayment mortgages.
- Suspended payments. This will only happen for a short period as the accumulated interest will be added to the mortgage debt.
- Extend the mortgage terms. Most lenders are quite happy to extend the repayment term of a mortgage which means that the monthly repayments will be smaller. If you have say a twenty-five year term, this could be extended to thirty or even thirty-five years, depending on your age and circumstances.
- With endowment mortgages, you always have to pay the life policy premiums. If you cannot afford both mortgage interest and premiums, it could be the time to change to an ordinary repayment mortgage.
- If you are unemployed, you may be eligible for supplementary benefit and have the cost of your mortgage interest paid by the state. Recent changes mean that only half the interest will be taken into account when assessing your benefit for the first sixteen weeks of the claim; previously the full amount was payable. After this period all mortgage interest due will be eligible for payment.

CHAPTER NINE:
A SHARE OF THE PROFIT

Britain is fast becoming a nation of shareholders, thanks largely to the Conservative party's privitisation programme and the massive increase in share prices over the last few years.

Buying shares

When you want to buy or sell shares, you have to deal with an authorised person such as a broker, bank or licensed dealer. Always remember to specify the number of shares you want to buy. If you want to buy at a specific price, you should say so, or alternatively you can specify a price range, or if you want to buy regardlcss of the price you should tell your broker to buy 'at best'. This means the shares will be purchased at the best price available, regardless of how much they may have risen since you issued the instruction.

Remember if you do buy 'at best' you have no right of redress if the order goes through at a higher price than you wished, provided it was the best price the broker could obtain at the time.

Often the best approach is to place your order subject to a certain price ceiling. This way hopefully you will not get any shocks and your broker will be able to act swiftly for you. The broker should always report back to you once the deal has been struck and tell you the exact terms of the transaction.

Transaction costs

Up till October 1986, there was a fixed price agreement under which all brokers agreed to sell shares for a specific commission related to the size of the purchase. This has now been scrapped and prices vary considerably. Provincial brokers tend to be much cheaper than City ones. As well as the broker's commission, you will have to pay ½% stamp duty on purchases and VAT of 15% on top of the dealing fees – on both buy or sell orders. This is effectively a government tax on share purchases.

Paperwork

Within forty-eight hours of dealing, you should get a contract note spelling out how many shares you have bought or sold, the price and charges involved. Keep this somewhere safe as you will need it when filling in your tax return.

You may have to wait for several weeks, or even months before you are sent a share certificate from the company's registrar. However, do not worry, your contract note is legal proof of ownership.

New issues

A new issue is the term given to shares sold to the public for the first time. Buying a new issue is rather like a lottery, there is no guarantee that your cheque and application will be picked, and you have no right to complain if your application is not successful. The shares are usually keenly priced to encourage investors as the aim of the issue is to ensure that all the shares are purchased. You can apply for shares in a new issue by filling out an application form. You will find these in newspapers, if it is a large issue, or they can be obtained from the company itself and its bankers. While many investors have made quick profits with new issues, particularly government ones, they are not a guaranteed route to instant riches.

If your application is successful you will receive an allotment letter from the company which will say how many shares you own. You do not have to pay any stamp duty or commission on the allotment letter and there is usually a reduced dealing charge when you want to sell.

If a new issue is substantially over-subscribed, that is there are applications for more shares than those issued, the company handling the flotation will sometimes decide to 'go to ballot'. Your application will go into a hat and if your form is pulled out, you will be allocated some shares.

Stock markets

Shares in a company are traded on a variety of markets in this country. These are:

- Stock Exchange

Only companies which have been carefully vetted and which meet the strictest conditions can have their shares traded on the London Stock Exchange. There are around 7,000 companies listed on the exchange and they all have to meet two main requirements. They must have a successful five year track record and they must sell at least 25% of the company's shares.

- Unlisted Securities Market

Newer and smaller companies can opt to have their shares traded on the Unlisted Securities Market. It is sometimes called the Stock Exchange's nursery as companies often go on to have their shares listed on the Stock Exchange. Companies only need a three year track record and are only required to sell 10% of their shares. However, they are vetted by the Stock Exchange just as thoroughly as if they were applying for a full listing.

- Over-The-Counter

You can also buy shares in companies not quoted on the Stock Exchange. The over-the-counter market (OTC) is run by dealers licensed by the Department of Trade and Industry as well as by members of Financial Intermediaries, Managers and Brokers Regulatory Association. They buy and sell shares direct to the public. The companies whose shares are traded in this way vary considerably in quality. Often only one dealer will make a price in the company's shares and investors sometimes find it difficult to sell shares traded on the OTC. At present there is no formal vetting procedure for companies who want their shares traded on the OTC, but there are plans to tighten up controls of this market. The Securities and Investment Board plans to impose onerous disclosure requirements on OTC traders if the shares are 'not marketable investments'. Under these rules firms will not be able to recommend shares which are difficult to trade without first giving clear warning to their customers that there may be problems when they wish to sell. Firms who recommend securities in this category will also be required to disclose their own holdings and forward sales of the shares. Also, when clients buy such securities the firm must reveal its mark-up, i.e. to distinguish between the price of the shares and the firm's commission.

• Third Tier

This is the most junior of the three markets set up by the Stock Exchange and is only designed for fledgling companies. It started trading in early 1987 and is designed to provided a well regulated alternative to the OTC. The types of company which qualify for the Third Tier market are those with at least one year's audited accounts and good earnings record; start ups which seem likely to make profits in their first year of trading and mineral exploration companies which have no profits record but were previously traded under Section 535 (3).

Shareholders' rights

When you invest money in a company, you become a shareholder and you actually own a part of the business. The directors who run the company are responsible for its day-to-day management, but as a shareholder you have a number of rights. These are:

• The right to a share of the profits known as a dividend. However, it is up to the directors to decide what, if any, dividends are to be paid. The directors announce a dividend, usually twice yearly, after they have calculated their half-year or end-year results. There is no automatic right to two dividends a year. If the directors decide the company is not trading profitably or a large cash sum is required for investment, they may not pay any dividends. In the past, the government has stepped in and restricted the growth in dividend payments. Dividends are paid net of basic rate tax. Non-tax payers can reclaim the tax deducted on their behalf from the Inland Revenue.

• The right to attend the annual general meeting, to raise any queries and to vote if a particular issue is bought up. Companies must give at least twenty-one day's notice of this meeting.

• The right to be sent a copy of the annual accounts and director's report each year. If you attend the annual general meeting you will be asked to approve the accounts, the appointment of the auditors and the election of directors.

- The right to appoint a proxy or stand-in to attend annual general meetings and vote on your behalf.
- You can combine with other shareholders, provided that together you own at least one-tenth of the company's paid up capital, and force the directors to hold an extraordinary general meeting if there is a contentious issue which you feel should be debated.
- If the company is wound up you have a right to a proportion of the remaining assets after creditors have been paid.
- You have the right to be consulted through a vote on all major changes of direction in the company's business. If, for example, the company is being taken-over, you will be able to vote for or against the proposal.

Raising cash

From time to time a company may decide that it needs to raise extra cash or to undertake a capital reconstruction. It might do one of the following:

- Bonus or scrip issues

If a company's share price has risen quickly, shareholders may be given a bonus or scrip issue. For example, one new share may be given for each existing share held. In theory in such a case the share price should halve, but in practice, it rarely falls by this much. However, companies usually decide to pay the same dividend, so existing shareholders receive twice as much income. This is usually enough to power the shares to greater heights.

- Rights issue

When a company wants to raise more money, it may decide to ask its own shareholders whether they are prepared to invest more money. Shareholders then have the right to buy new shares at a fixed price. The size of their holding will dictate how many new shares they have the right to apply for. Shareholders can either: take up their rights in full, sell the rights or take up some of the rights offered and sell the remainder.

Splitting the shares

You might be sent a letter telling you the company has decided to split its shares. Assuming the price is 100p, and it has decided to split each share into two the price should fall to 50p. You will receive a formal notification and you should put this document with your share certificate.

Capital reconstruction

If a company runs into financial difficulties, it will need to raise fresh capital. Often the bank or organisation lending it money will want an increased share in the business – and existing shareholders will have their holding diluted. Usually this is only undertaken as a 'last ditch' effort to stop the company going into liquidation. Shareholders should look on this as the better of two evils and vote accordingly.

Takeovers

Take-overs are normally good news for shareholders. The company making the bid will usually offer a price which is above the going market price and so you will make a profit. They cannot pay you a lower price than the sum they have paid for other shares in the past twelve months. If the offer is made by a company which already holds 15% of the takeover target's shares then they must provide you with a cash equivalent. You will be asked to vote on whether you think the take-over should proceed. The bidder needs approval from more than half of all the shareholders before it wins the battle. Make sure you check the voting deadline, usually its best to wait until the last minute before voting as sometimes higher bids come along.

Complaints

If you are unhappy about the way the company is being run, you should first of all write to its managing director. If that does not bring results, you can try writing to the Stock Exchange if its shares are traded on one of the three markets under its control or the Department of Trade and Industry if you think the directors may have breached company law. The last resort is to sell the shares.

Dealing on equal terms

The Stock Exchange's aim is to make sure all shareholders are on an equal footing and can trade on the basis of the same information. For this reason, the Stock Exchange reserves the right to stop or suspend trading in a particular company's shares. It will do this if it feels some important information is about to be released and news leaks out before a formal announcement is made. It could be that the directors of a company are about to undertake a capital reconstruction or announce details of a take-over bid. You will not be able to sell your shares or buy any new ones while the quotation is suspended. Normally the suspension is only for a short while.

Concert party

If two or more shareholders get together and are regarded as acting 'in concert' they have to abide by Take Over Panel rules. This panel supervises the conduct of anyone who buys large numbers of shares in a company which is quoted on the Stock Exchange. It lays down a strict code of conduct.

- Parties acting in concert must have their shareholdings added together and the relevant details made public if they exceed 5%.
- If 'holdings' of people acting together total more than 29.9%, they have to bid for the rest of the shares at a price at least equal to the highest price paid within the last twelve months and must provide a cash alternative to any share offer.

Insider dealing

You cannot use privileged information to make money on share deals. For example, an employee of a company may know that profits have jumped dramatically and that these figures will be announced to the public in a couple of weeks or that a take-over bid is in the offing. He or she must not use this information to make profits by dealing in the company's shares. Similarly this information must not be passed on to a third party who may in turn use it to make money by trading in the company's shares.

Share Package Deals

Many people have become interested in investing in the stockmarket as a result of the massive advertising campaign surrounding the sale of British Telecom, British Gas, British Airways and a number of private companies, such as Virgin Airways, to the public over the past few years. Yet few people have the time, experience or desire to pick their own shares and therefore they turn to the professionals to look after their money for them. The law lays down strict rules about who is qualified to take on this task and the regulations they must comply with are very detailed and designed to ensure investors are protected wherever feasible from poor management, sloppy administration and fraud. Although, unfortunately no government has yet designed a set of rules that can stop the determined fraudster.

Authorised unit trusts

The Department of Trade and Industry is responsible for policing the unit trust industry. It sets rules on the type, size and quality of companies who can offer authorised unit trusts to the public, vets each trust to see it complies with the general rules and in return gives the unit trust company considerable freedom to market the fund to the general public. Under the Financial Services Act some constraints on the unit trust group's marketing activities will be imposed via the newly set up self-regulatory body, the Life Assurance and Unit Trust Regulatory Association. Overall these are designed to protect would-be investors from being sold unit trusts on the basis of over optimistic promises and to give potential customers the opportunity to change their minds in those situations where they may have been pressurised into making a hasty investment.

You have the right to know:

- Investment policy
- Gross yield on the fund
- Charges, both current and the potential increase which the managers can pay themselves without seeking the comment of unit holders.

You also have the right:

- To change your mind within fourteen days and decide not

to go ahead with your investment if you have been cold called. This right will be introduced late in 1987.

- To sell your units at any time.
- To receive twice yearly information about the trust's portfolio.

You can buy units over the phone, either direct from the company itself or through a broker, or alternatively by filling in an application form. You will be allocated units at the offer price ruling at the time your request was received. Within a few days you will receive a note informing you of the purchase details, which you should keep for tax purposes. Several weeks later the trust company's registrar, often the trust group itself, will send you a formal certificate. This should be dispatched within four weeks but recently some groups have been sending out certificates months later as they cannot cope with the influx of new investors.

The rules governing how unit trust companies price their units were changed in 1988. Under the new rules in force from July 1, 1988 companies can choose whether to deal on the previous day's price, known as historic prices or to deal on a forward basis, with orders transacted at the next determined price. If the fund value does move by more than 2%, the managers must either revalue the units or move to forward pricing.

Under the new regulations unit trust information in newspapers must show three prices – offer, bid and cancellation at the most recent valuation available with the actual spread used for deals. They must also show the initial change in percentage form at least once a week. On deals of more than £15,000 managers can deal outside the spread, provided the price is still within permitted limits or deal on a forward-pricing basis. Companies will have a one-week settlement period.

One of the key factors about unit trusts is that an independent trustee, normally a large insurance company or bank, keeps an eagle eye on the unit trust manager's activities to make sure no rules are breached and that investors' interests are protected. In the past, the trustee tended to adopt a low key approach but there are signs that under the new self-regulatory regime they will play an increasingly active role.

Before managers make a major switch of investment policy or merge their trusts with another, they will require consent from unit holders. They have to give you twenty-one days' notice of the meeting and then need a majority of 75%. Depending on the trust deed, anything from 10% up to 50% must vote. No such restrictions are imposed on any manager before they sell a unit trust to another group, provided of course that group is authorised by the Department of Trade and Industry to run unit trusts.

Complaints

If you think the managers are not sticking to the investment criteria laid down in the trust deed, you should first talk to the trustees. If that does not bring satisfaction, then try the Unit Trust Association which is the trade body for unit trusts. The last port of call is the Department of Trade and Industry.

If you are unhappy with the performance, you can take it up with the fund managers. If they do not give you a satisfactory response, you can contact the Investment Management Regulatory Organisation, the self-regulatory organisation to which all investment managers have to belong. However, you must remember that any investment in equities involves risk and units can fall in price as well as rise. It is also best to consider them as long-term investments, not judge them on a monthly basis.

If your certificate has not come through in a reasonable length of time, contact the registrar. If that does not bring results, try the trustee. If you feel that an advertisement placed by a unit trust company is misleading, inaccurate or unsuitable, first talk to the Unit Trust Association who has to vet all advertisements placed by unit trust companies. You can also try the Advertising Standards Authority and Department of Trade and Industry.

A new arm of the insurance ombudsman bureau will be set up during 1988 which will cover the unit trust business of Lantro members who care to join. The unit trust ombudsman will have a wide brief covering both 'good investment and good marketing practices' and be in a position to make cash awards of up to £100,000 to aggrieved customers who can prove their case.

Unauthorised unit trusts

These are trusts which have not been authorised by the Department of Trade and Industry and are therefore not free to seek cash from UK investors except through authorised brokers, whose responsibility is to protect their clients' interests. Your rights will vary in each trust and you should check out the fund manager with care.

Investment trusts

An investment trust is in fact as company whose business is to invest in other companies. Some investment trusts are private companies owned by families and their shares are not sold to the public. Other investment trusts, often run by major financial companies, have a quote on the London Stock Exchange. They are vetted by the Stock Exchange and have to comply with rules under The Companies Act 1981. You can buy shares in investment trusts traded on the stock market in the same way as if you were buying shares in any other company.

Investment trusts do not have to pay tax on capital gains realised provided they meet three main requirements:

- they must be based in the UK.
- they must get most of their income from stocks and shares listed on the Stock Exchange.
- they must not distribute capital gains to shareholders. Income earned by the trust's investments is usually paid out to shareholders twice a year, less any expenses incurred.

They are not allowed to invest more than 15% of their assets in any one company. Companies that want to become members of the Association of Investment Trust Companies must invest at least 60% of their assets in stocks and shares quoted on the Stock Exchange. The Association of Investment Trust Companies sponsor a helpful guide called 'More Shares for Your Money', published by Rosters, which costs £5.95. It also gives a list of stockbrokers willing to take on new investment trust business.

You have the right to know:

- investment philosophy and vote on any major changes

- the names and background of the company's directors but not the people who are actually choosing the investments.

  The directors are free to delegate this to the people or company they feel will do the best job.

The directors of the investment trust are free to decide the company's dividend policy and have a duty to run the company efficiently. As a shareholder you will be consulted on matters of major policy changes, acquisitions or disposals, say if the trust is the subject of a takeover or wishes to merge with another trust. You can attend annual general meetings or send a proxy to vote on your behalf. If you are unhappy with the way the company is run then if you can persuade 10% of the shareholders to support you, you can force an extraordinary general meeting.

Personal equity plans

First introduced on January 1, 1987 these are tax free plans where the bulk of your money is invested in British companies quoted on the London stock exchange and the Unlisted Securities Market. Under the new investor protection framework due to come into force in January 1988 these plans are treated as management agreements. This means that people selling the plans have to make sure this is a suitable investment for you and to inform you of the risks associated with each plan.

As well as the general rules governing management agreements the government when it set up these plans laid down a number of rights which planholders must enjoy. These include:

- the opportunity to receive the annual report and accounts of each company in which your money is invested.
- the opportunity to exercise your rights as a shareholder by attending meetings and voting on important decisions – but you might have to pay an extra fee.
- the right to enjoy all the proceeds of the plan, both profits and income, free of tax provided you leave your money invested for a full calendar year and that none of the government's regulations on the manner the plan should be administered have been breached.

There are basically two types of plans, advisory ones where

you make the investment decisions and discretionary ones, where the plan manager chooses the shares. Whoever is in the hot seat they have to comply with the following obligations:

- There are strict rules about the price at which your money is invested. The Inland Revenue insist that all investments must be made at open market prices so no false gains are created.
- Any cash in the plan must be placed in a special deposit account which pays gross interest and which cannot be mixed with the manager's own funds.
- The rules on liquidity and investment criteria.
- Restrictions on withdrawals in order to qualify for tax-relief.

Unlike unit trusts and life assurance policies there is no cooling off period, so make sure you give yourself plenty of time to think through your decision before investing. You are free to cash in your plan at any time but if you do so before a full calendar year has elapsed you may end up with a tax bill and will probably pay an exit fee to the plan manager. Under the government's rules you are free to transfer your plan to another recognised plan manager at any time without generating a tax bill but you may find your original plan manager charges you an administration fee for this.

While authorised unit trusts incorporate a double tier of protection for the investor this is not the case with personal equity plans, which therefore require additional care on the part of the investor. First, only sizeable companies who pass muster with the Department of Trade and Industry can sell unit trusts while any company authorised to sell shares to the public can register with the Inland Revenue as a personal equity plan manager. Second, the trustee of an authorised unit trust is in a prime position to make sure the managers are sticking to their agreed task and that funds are being used for the appropriate purpose. There is no such watchdog in the case of personal equity plans, although the Inland Revenue insist that all shareholdings must be identified as the customer's not the manager's.

Under the general rules governing management agreements all share dealings must be at the best market price and reported immediately to the customer. This latter rule is being waived for plan managers when they are running discretionary plans which are invested in top companies quoted on the London stock exchange. They need only report to their customers on a quarterly basis.

SHARE PACKAGE DEALS AT A GLANCE

	Unit Trusts	Unauthorised Unit Trusts	Quoted Investment Trusts	Personal Equity Plans
Who regulates them	Department of Trade and Industry Securities and Investment Board*	Foreign governments	Stock Exchange Department of Trade and Industry	Securities and Investment Board*
Cooling-off period	Yes, if sold as a result of a cold-call†	No	No	No
Pricing	At manager's discretion within boundaries of Department of Trade and Industry formula	At manager's discretion	Determined by market force	Value of plan reflects the value of underlying holdings exactly
Investment constraints	Money must be invested in shares, gilts or convertibles of the type or country specified in the trust deed	At manager's discretion. Usually free to include shares, gifts, bonds, currencies and physical assets	According to company's articles of association. No restrictions imposed on type of investment per se, ie can include unquoted shares, physical assets and company may borrow	Laid down by Inland Revenue. 75% in approved UK shares with rest in unit trusts or investment trusts. Strict rules to limit uninvested cash
Who makes the investment decision	The UK fund manager with the assistance of an adviser if wished	The fund manager	The director's or their appointed staff	The customer, the plan manager or an appointed investment manager
Where can they be bought	Either from the unit trust group direct, an authorised investment adviser, or via a coupon in an advertisement or leaflet	From an authorised investment adviser after a full consultation	From an authorised share dealer	Direct from the plan manager, an authorised investment adviser or by filling in the appropriate coupon

NOTES:–*When the rules concerning management agreements under the Financial Services Act 1986 are brought into force, later this year.

†Cooling-off period due to be introduced under the terms of the Financial Services Act, in July.

CHAPTER TEN: INSURANCE AND PENSIONS

Insurance is something that concerns everyone at some stage in their lives. The idea is to protect yourself and your assets against financial loss. You make a contract with an insurance company to pay money, called a premium, and in return the insurance company promises to pay you money if the loss happens. You can insure against almost any loss imaginable. Film stars have insured their legs, zoos their star gorilla and singers their voices. However, it is not a form of gambling. In order to buy insurance you must have what is called an 'insurable interest'. In other words, the film star can insure her own legs, but a friend who thinks there is a sporting chance the actress might have a bad accident and seriously injure her legs cannot take out insurance. If you are organising a summer fete, and you would lose money if it rained, then you can buy insurance to cover that eventuality.

Buying procedures

When you take out any kind of an insurance policy, you have to fill in a proposal form. The company will look at your answers and decide whether you are a reasonable risk, whether they should charge a higher premium, or turn you down altogether. It is up to them to make a commercial decision based on the hard facts you supply. You have no right to object or to redress if they refuse to insure you.

You must supply all the information required. Do not be tempted to give evasive answers. If the insurance company finds you have been untruthful or have withheld relevant information, it is within its rights to refuse to pay out on your claim.

You also have a duty throughout the life of the policy to tell the insurance company if your circumstances have changed in any way which would affect that policy. Once the insurance company has accepted your proposal, you have to pay your premium, whether it is monthly or annually. If you do forget to make a payment, the insurance company has the right to cancel your cover – and will not have to pay out if you claim. Do be careful around renewal time – most companies send out renewal reminders a month or so before the expiry date so pay up on time or arrange alternative cover.

You can buy insurance to cover all sort of eventualities, such as:

- Car insurance
- Holiday insurance
- Hospital cash plans
- Home contents/all risks
- House buildings insurance
- Jury service
- Multiple births
- Permanent health insurance
- Personal accident insurance
- Pet insurance
- Private health insurance
- Warranty insurance
- Weather 'pluvius' policies

Car insurance

You must have some insurance cover when you drive a car, otherwise you are breaking the law. The minimum insurance cover required by law is called Road Traffic Act cover and it pays out if you injure other people. There are three other types of motor insurances: third party only; third party fire and theft, and fully comprehensive.

Each provides a different level of cover so make sure you know what you are buying. The widest and most expensive cover is provided by what is called a fully comprehensive policy. If your car has a reasonable value and you can afford to do so, it is always worth taking out this type of cover. It pays out for damage to your car as well as others and it does not matter how this damage is incurred.

If you have an old banger, third party fire and theft which

is cheaper may be sufficient. Remember, if you drive when disqualified from doing so, any insurance cover is automatically invalid.

Holiday insurance

There is no law which says you must buy holiday insurance but as the risk of a claim is quite high you would be foolish not to do so. A few small tour operators, usually offering ski holidays insist you take their insurance and they are legally entitled to do this. A good holiday insurance policy will cover you against flight delays, loss of baggage and personal possessions, medical costs if you are ill or injured, loss of money, personal accident cover, will pay out if you have to cancel the holiday unexpectedly, or if you have to fly home because of illness or death. Do watch out for policies which exclude pregnant ladies or those people with certain medical conditions.

Home contents

While the company providing your mortgage will insist that you take out house buildings insurance, you do not have to take out cover for your possessions. However, do not skip this otherwise if a thief breaks in, or there is fire you will not get any compensation for the loss of your possessions. You should value everything in your home and take out cover for the sum it would cost to replace your belongings. Fixed items, like fitted kitchen units, cupboards, but not carpets, come under buildings insurance rather than contents. The rule to keep in mind is that anything you would normally take with you when selling the house comes under the 'contents' label.

There are two or three different types of cover for contents. They range in price from the most expensive 'new for old' under which you obtain the replacement value of the goods lost or stolen, to the most basic 'indemnity' under which you would be given the value of the goods, less wear and tear.

If you under-insure your contents, you run the risk of your insurance company scaling down any claim that you make by the same proportion as you have underinsured. You should increase the value of your contents cover each year in line with the cost of living and remember to add in additions made throughout the year. Individual items of particular value should be insured through your contents policy but listed separately with a stated value. Most policies limit the sum they pay out per item to around £500, unless you have insured the high value items specially.

Hospital cash plans

These will pay out if you have to spend a time as a patient in hospital. They will give you a flat sum of so many pounds per night while you are in hospital. Most plans only pay out for a specific period after a certain time has elapsed and you can usually reduce the cost by opting for plans which only pay out after one month. These are not a substitute for private health insurance, but can provide useful income cushion if you do have to go into hospital for a longish period.

House buildings insurance

If you have a mortgage you will have to insure your home. You have the right to choose your own insurance company and although the company lending you the money to buy the house usually suggests a short list of potential insurers, you are free to choose your own company. Some building societies and banks have organised package deals with insurers. These can be good value, so its worth checking out the financial facts and figures. Remember also that a bank or building society which does a great deal of business with an insurance company is often in a strong position when trying to get a claim settled speedily and in full.

You have to insure your home for what it would cost to re-build it. This is not the same figure as the price you paid for the home. However, if say your home was partially destroyed by fire then you would have to pay demolition costs as well as the cost of rebuilding. The time to buy home buildings insurance is when you exchange contracts. Do not wait until the purchase is complete as once you have exchanged contracts you are responsible for the state of the house.

The insurance company will pay out if you have burst pipes, leaking roofs, etc., but they will usually expect you to pay the first part of a claim, perhaps the first £15 or £20. This is called 'the excess' and should be clearly stated in your policy.

Jury service

If you are on the electoral role, you might be selected for jury service and unless you have a very good reason for not attending, you will have to do it. If you could suffer financial loss through having to do jury service, you can take out an insurance policy which will pay you a cash sum if you are selected. The self-employed should produce a letter from their accountant showing the likely short-fall.

Multiple births

One baby is quite expensive, two or more can be horrific. If you want to insure against having twins, triplets, etc., you must take out the insurance cover soon after you know you are pregnant and before a doctor could tell how many babies you are likely to have. If there is a history of twins in your family, the premium might be quite hefty, or the insurance company might even refuse to give you cover.

Permanent health insurance

This should really be called permanent ill-health insurance, as it pays you a continuing income if you are unable to work because of illness or injury. Self-employed people can take out individual policies, while employees should check to see if their company has such a scheme. Self-employed people will have to give details of their health and might have to pay a higher premium if they have had medical problems in the past.

Personal accident

This will pay out a lump sum if you have an accident. For example, if you were involved in a motoring accident and suffered permanent injury then you can claim under this policy.

Pet insurance

If you have a sick cat or dog, or even a horse, veterinary bills can be very costly. This insurance policy will cover the costs of vet's fees – usually up to a maximum sum each year. It will also pay towards advertising costs if your pet goes missing and even a cash sum if your pet dies through injury or sickness.

Pluvius cover

If you are organising an event like a summer fete which would suffer financially because of the rain, then you can take out special insurance which will pay out a cash sum to compensate for the money you have lost because of the inclement weather. This is known as 'pluvius' after the Latin for rain.

Private health insurance

If you are not keen to rely entirely on the National Health Service, but can't afford private medical treatment, you can take out private health insurance. There are half a dozen companies offering schemes and premiums which will vary depending on what type of hospital you want to be treated in and your age. If for example, you and your wife live in London and are in your forties with two children and are treated in a London teaching hospital, you will have to pay the most expensive premium perhaps as much as £90 a month. Elsewhere, medical costs are lower and you will pay a smaller premium in the £35 to £45 a month region. The plans cover all medical treatment when you are in hospital, and various out-patient treatment. They do not cover the cost of going to see a private general practitioner. Also, your general practitioner must recommend that you need treatment and will have to sign a form saying that he recommends such treatment. There is a set scale of fees they are prepared to cover for any given operation.

Warranty insurance

When you buy new white or brown goods, you will notice most are guaranteed for one year. If you want to extend that guarantee for a further two or four years, then you can usually do so by taking out warranty insurance. However, do not expect every fault to be covered, read the fine prints carefully to see what exclusions the company make. Most exclude wear and tear for example.

LIFE ASSURANCE

The old adage that life assurance is sold not bought rings true. It is associated with doom and gloom and few of us enjoy thinking about our future demise. The onus is very much on the salesman to convince the prospective punter. There is a saying that if you can sell life insurance, you can sell anything.

The choice

- Term assurance

  The simplest and cheapest form of life assurance. You pay a monthly or annual premium for a specified term, i.e. number of years. If you die your dependants will be paid a cash sum but if you survive you will not receive any pay-out.

- Whole life

  As the name implies, you pay premiums for the whole of your life and when you die your dependants receive the cash sum which has been built up by investing your premiums. If you want to stop paying premiums when you retire, you can choose a 'limited payment policy'. As there is a guaranteed pay-out, albeit at an unspecified date in the future, premiums are higher than for term assurance.

- Endowment assurance

  You pay premiums for a specified time, normally between ten and fifty years. Your money is invested by the insurance company. If you die during the period of the loan your dependants get a lump sum, while if you survive you will collect the proceeds. There are two types of endowment policies – either with-profits or without-profits. Under a with-profit policy you receive a guaranteed sum and your share of any profits made by the life assurance company. If you opt for the cheaper without-profits you only receive the guaranteed sum.

- Investment linked insurance

  Part of the premium gives you life cover whilst the remainder is invested in a separate fund. This can be a unit trust or an insurance fund. Life cover will be fixed at a guaranteed sum but the value of the investment part at the end of the policy depends very much on the fund's performance.

Estimated returns

In order to persuade you to buy an insurance policy, the salesman tries to make the package as attractive as possible. However, they cannot promise that the insurance company will do absolute wonders when they invest your money. Under new rules introduced in 1987, companies selling pension and life assurance plans must all use the same growth rates when estimating your future return on a policy. On pension plans the figure is 13% gross a year. On life assurance policies this return is reduced to 10.75%, after tax.

Insurable interest

You can direct that the proceeds of your life insurance policy are paid to anyone you like. However, you can only insure the life of another person if you have a financial interest in that person's death or survival. A parent may not insure the life of a child – except for a small policy to pay for burial costs – but a lender may insure the life of his debtor since he stands to suffer a loss if the borrower dies. Also a woman can insure her ex-husband if, say, he pays her maintenance and she would suffer financially if he were to die. If you are getting divorced you should make sure your solicitor takes the value of any life insurance and pension policies into account when splitting up the matrimonial assets.

Suicide

Some life insurance companies have a suicide clause in their policy document and will not pay out if the policyholder commits suicide within a specified period of taking out the policy. This is typically one year.

Equality

Life insurance is not covered by the sex equality legislation – and that is good news for women as they pay lower premiums than men. This is because most statistics show that women live on average around five years longer than men. What most life insurance companies do is to have one set of premium figures based on charges for men, and then quote a premium rate for a woman that is the equivalent of a man four or five years younger.

Proposal form

Once you have decided to take out an insurance contract, you have to fill in a proposal form. You will have to provide various personal details, including age, marital status, health record and work. Take your time and be sure all the questions are answered truthfully and in full. Never just sign a form completed by your broker or a salesman. It is up to you to include any fact which might materially affect the insurance company's decision on whether to accept your business. In practice, this is very difficult for the layman to know but vital as most insurance companies will not pay out on claims if they can prove you either gave false or incomplete information. If in doubt ask.

Insurance companies calculate the amount they charge people who want to buy life assurance cover according to age, normally at your next birthday. Except on simplified forms you will usually be asked to name your doctor, who may be approached to give details of your medical history.

Under new rules brought in by the Financial Services Act 1986, anyone buying an insurance policy with an investment element has the option to cancel within fourteen days of purchase and get a full refund of cash paid.

Medicals

Insurance companies sometimes insist you have a medical before they agree to take you on as a policyholder. If you are over sixty they nearly always insist on a medical, also when you are taking out a policy with a large guaranteed sum, say over £50,000. If the insurer classifies you as what is called an 'impaired life' – i.e. your medical record is not brilliant and your life expectancy is below average, they may still agree to accept your application but charge a higher than normal premium.

Most life insurance companies are now including a question on AIDS which reads somthing like this: 'Have you ever received or considered you ought to seek medical advice regarding AIDS?'. Companies often ask unmarried men to have blood tests to check for AIDS depending on the sum insured.

Occupation

They may refuse to insure you, or charge an extra premium if you have what is termed a 'risky occupation'. This includes miners, deep-sea divers, publicans, steeplejacks and jockeys. There is nothing you can do about this, except ask your broker to introduce you to companies who specialise in insurance for people in your profession. If you regularly undertake a hazardous recreational hobby – like mountaineering, flying, gliding or rally driving, you might also find your premium is loaded.

Under cover

You are only officially insured once the company has accepted your proposal and you have paid the first premium. In the case of off-the-page advertisements you are insured once you have paid the premium.

If you fall behind on your payments you usually have a few days grace although this depends on how often you pay your premium. For annual premiums, you usually have thirty days leeway but for monthly premiums it is usually between seven and fifteen days. You are still insured during the grace period, but after that if you have not paid you no longer have any right to claim under the policy. Companies can, if they wish, make the policy paid-up, which means no further payments are made. If you are prepared to start paying the premiums again they may revive the policy after you have paid the outstanding instalments, interest charges and an administrative fee.

Some insurance companies will insist that women produce both a birth and wedding certificate when taking out an insurance policy. They want to make absolutely sure that you are who you say you are. Similarly with a claim they may ask for both certificates – otherwise there may be a delay. Claims on life assurance policies have to be supported by death certificates, again to minimise fraud.

Safety

Under the terms of the Policyholders Protection Act, 1975 policyholders in any insurance company that goes bust are guaranteed up to 90% of the benefits to which they are entitled.

This scheme is not affected by the Financial Services Act. However under the act, you will also be protected if the broker or adviser to whom you sent a cheque for your premiums subsequently goes bust without forwarding your cheque to the appropriate life company. You will be repaid in full provided the sum does not exceed £30,000. You get 100% of the first £30,000 and 90% of the next £20,000 making a total of £48,000. This provision of the act comes into force in July 1988.

Repayment difficulties

More than half of all life assurance policies taken out are surrendered before the maturity date. If you do find you cannot afford to continue paying the premiums, you may be tempted to cash it in early. However, this can be an expensive mistake, particularly in the first five or so years of the policy when you may not even receive the value of your original premiums – let alone any profits. Also, if you took the policy out before March 14, 1984 you will be enjoying tax relief of 12½% on your premiums, a concession which is no longer available on new policies.

If you cannot afford or no longer wish to pay premiums each month, you usually have several alternatives:

- Make the policy paid up. You stop paying the premiums, but leave your cash in the life assurance fund. This way you will keep bonuses earned to date and usually collect a proportion of future bonuses, including the final bonus.
- Ask if you can have a policy loan. Many insurance companies will lend you money against the security of your policy at an attractive interest rate. They will only do so when your policy has acquired a surrender value and typically you can borrow up to 90% of the surrender value. While you will have to pay interest regularly, you don't have to repay the capital until the policy matures in which case the sum owing is just deducted from the final payout.
- Partial surrender
  You collect only a proportion of the cash-in-value and go on paying a similarly reduced proportion of the premium. At maturity you receive the same reduced proportion of the final payout.

Surrender

If you decide you want to surrender, write to the company and ask how much you will receive. Unfortunately there is nothing you can do to force the company to pay you more if you think they are being mean. However, under new rules introduced by the Financial Services Act 1986 salesmen have to tell potential customers how much they would receive if they cashed in the policy during the first five years.

The right policy

Whether an insurance adviser is independent or tied to a particular company, he still earns commission on the policies he sells. The bigger the policy, the more he earns. It is surprising how many people with investment linked insurance believe that they have bought more life cover than they actually receive. They have been convinced by a smooth talking salesman that this is the right thing for them. Remember that commission on investment and endowment plans is much higher than on term or basic whole life policies.

There is no such thing as the one perfect plan for everyone with life insurance. You have to select according to your particular circumstances. In general terms, the younger you are, the more emphasis you should place on protective insurance. You will probably have less money to play with and any surplus will normally go on the house and family. As you get older, so the emphasis will shift and investment will take a higher priority.

Before you sign up for any investment linked insurance, take a close look at the charges structure. You should expect to see a small percentage of your premium deducted for general expenses, and there will be an annual charge on the value of the units – normally between ½% and 1½%. Watch out for the funds that allocate special capital or initial units in the first few years. These may incur additional charges each year for the life of the policy and can add up to a great deal of money over the years.

Helpful associations

- The Association of British Insurers – the principal trade association in the British insurance industry with over 400 member companies. It produces various leaflets about insurance and will look into complaints about members.

- The Associated Scottish Life Offices – set up by the Scottish Life Assurance offices it is a trade association for Scottish insurers.
- The Life Insurance Council – operates as part of the ABI dealing with life insurance.
- The Life Insurance Association – it has four main functions: promote communications, improve business standards, sponsor courses and lectures and to liaise with the government.
- The Financial Intermediaries, Managers and Brokers Regulatory Association. This is a second line of defence if the policy was sold by one of their members.
- Life Assurance and Unit Trust Regulatory Association. They can be approached if you have any complaints about the marketing literature on a product or if you were sold the policy by a life assurance company salesman.
- Investment Management Regulatory Association. They can be contacted over investment problems.
- BIIBA – British Insurance and Investment Brokers Association – a trade body for brokers in both the insurance and investment field.
- IBRC – Insurance Brokers Registration Council – has applied for Recognised Public Body Status and will licence members to give investment advice under the Financial Services Act.

PENSIONS

Pensions have been a political football for some time. Now that we have a Tory government for the next four years, the Thatcherite reforms are heading straight for their goal. Their aim is to encourage everyone to provide for their own future with less reliance on the state. Certainly the old age pension will not be enough. The gap between this and actual earnings is widening all the time and unless you have an additional pension when you retire, you are likely to suffer a big drop in your living standards.

The cornerstone of Tory policy is that everyone with sufficient income will be able to buy a personal pension plan. Life insurance companies used to do most of the pension business but now the banks, unit trusts and building societies are getting in on the act. There are a great number of people out there who will be only too willing to sell you a pension policy.

Pensions have always been a complex subject and during this transitional period, they are even more difficult to understand. That old Latin saying 'caveat emptor' – let the buyer beware – has never been more applicable.

What the state provides

- The basic state pension is paid to people who have clocked up sufficient National Insurance contributions. Men qualify at 65 and women at age 60.
- Since 1978 there has been a second tier of state pension, called the state earning related pension scheme – SERPS for short. This can give you an additional pension of up to 25% of your average earnings over a 20 year period (within certain band limits).
- The present government plans to reduce this extra pension to 20% of average earnings because it believes the country cannot afford to pay an ever increasing number of pensioners at the former rates.

Contracting out

Private pension schemes which meet the government's requirements can opt out of the SERPS scheme. This means that both employer and employee pay substantially less National Insurance contribution.

Private pensions

These are often called occupational pensions. The most common relate to your salary in the two or three years before retirement – final salary schemes. A typical scheme would provide:

- One sixtieth of final salary for each year of service up to forty years, i.e. a maximum pension of 2/3rds of final salary which is the ceiling permitted by the Inland Revenue.
- On the death of the member, half the existing pension or future pension is paid to the widow.

- A further lump sum of up to four times salary can be paid to the widow on the death of the member.
- Part of the pension may be commuted for a lump sum at retirement which is totally tax free.

In addition some employers provide what is called a money purchase scheme. This gives an individual pension account which you can identify as your own. However, it does not guarantee the amount of your pension which will relate to the fund's performance.

One of the biggest changes on the pension scene is that from April 1988 membership of a company or occupational pension scheme is no longer compulsory. If you wish you can opt out of your employer's scheme and set up your own personal pension. This can be particularly good for people who change jobs frequently. You will have your own pot of money which you can take with you. Older people who plan to stay with the firm are probably better advised to keep going with the company scheme.

If you leave your job you must be offered a preserved pension provided you have completed at least two full years service. Since 1st January 1985, preserved benefits have to be increased by 5% per annum or by the Retail Price Index figure if this is less.

Tax advantages

Under current rules, occupational pension schemes have considerable tax advantages. These include:

- Tax relief is obtained at the highest rate paid on the employer's and employee's contributions up to certain limits.
- The employer's contribution is not taxed as a benefit in kind.
- The funds grow free of all income and capital gains tax.
- Tax free lump sums are available on death and retirement up to limits set out by the Inland Revenue.

Additional voluntary contributions

An occupation scheme may be non-contributory, in which case the employer pays all the costs, or contributory, where the costs are shared with the employee. Employees have the right to contribute higher amounts to take advantage of the generous tax reliefs available and secure extra benefits. You may pay up to 15% of your salary into the pension fund and that includes any contributions to the main scheme as well as your voluntary top-ups. These extra payments are known as AVCs, additional voluntary contributions. However you must ensure that your total benefits do not exceed Inland Revenue maxima.

- From April 1987 they may only be used to provide extra pension and life cover, not lump sums.
- Pre April 1987 policies can still be used for lump sums.
- Provided your pension scheme will allow it, you can pay in variable amounts and alter the timing each year as much as you like.
- You can now invest in a company of your own choice – a free standing AVC – rather than stay with the scheme organised by your employer.

Personal pensions

Nearly half the 21m employees in Britain are not in any sort of occupational pension scheme. In addition, there are some 2.5m self employed persons who have no pension other than the basic state pension. Until recently they have been able to take out a retirement annuity with similar tax concessions to occupational schemes. However, from the 1st July 1988 the floodgate will be opened on personal pensions. Their main features are:

- The pension belongs to you alone and is portable – you can take it with you from job to job.
- Up to 17.5% of earnings can be paid into a scheme, more if you are over 50. Full tax relief is granted on the amount.
- Personal pensions may be provided by banks, building societies, unit trusts and friendly societies as well as life insurance companies.
- Benefits may be taken at any time between ages fifty and seventy-five.
- You may contract out of the state earnings related pension

scheme. In this case an amount equal to the savings in employer's and employee's National Insurance contributions involved when contracting-out of a final salary scheme, will be paid by the DHSS into your personal pension. Contracting-out can be backdated to April 1987 and an incentive of 2% of earnings for up to six years will also be paid by the DHSS. Benefits in respect of these contributions must be taken at state pension age.

- Your contributions will be net of basic rate tax. The tax relief will be claimed directly from the Inland Revenue.
- Employers may contribute part of the 17½% but are not obliged to do so.
- One quarter of the fund may be taken as a tax free lump sum at retirement subject to a maximum ceiling which is currently £150,000. The rest must be taken as a pension. Any fund from contributions paid by the DHSS can only be taken as a pension.
- Your personal pension plan will be free of all taxes.

Pension mortgages

The ability to take part of your pension entitlement as a tax-free lump sum on retirement has led to a number of companies offering interest-only pension mortgages. These are similar in principle to endowment mortgages, but the loan is paid back when you retire out of the pension lump sum. The cash may come from an occupational scheme, an old AVC arrangement, or one of the new personal pensions.

You get tax relief on both your pension contributions and the interest on the loan (up to £30,000). However your ultimate pension will be less as part of the lump sum will go to pay off the mortgage. In addition, the government has now reduced the maximum lump sum payable under each pension plan to £150,000.

Pension posers

With so many companies offering such a wide range of policies, you are bound to be thoroughly confused. Not all plans are the same. Investment returns will vary. They will all have different levels of expenses which will be deducted from your contributions. In addition the general terms and conditions will vary. Professional advice is certainly needed but here are a few pointers.

- Although future projections must be made on a standardised basis, by all companies, check on the returns over the last few years.
- A large part of the expenses is taken out by agent's commission. How much is involved? What are the other charges?
- Plans are in two tiers. The first tier allows you to contract out of the state SERPS scheme, and will not be worth much commission to the agent. The second tier gives you your extra pension and will be the icing on the cake for the agent. Do not be talked into paying out more than you can afford.
- Some companies do not pay commission to agents. Are their terms any better?
- When you sign up for a personal pension contract, you will get a cooling off notice which gives you fourteen days to change your mind. This notice will show transfer values over the first five years using standard returns but using the companies own charging structure. A plan with lower expenses in the first five years will show higher values – normally a plus point. Beware the front end loaders – the pension provider which takes the bulk of its charges in the first few years. These will reduce the returns quite considerably.
- One of the latest trends is towards policy fees. On the face of it they are quite small – say £1 a month. If these fees are charged on an increasing basis, in line with the Retail Prices Index, they can reduce the value of your fund by a considerable amount.

USEFUL ADDRESSES

Advertising Standards
Authority (ASA)
Brook House
2-16 Torrington Place
London WC1E 7HN
Tel: (01) 580 5555

Associated Scottish Life Offices
23 St. Andrews Square
Edinburgh EH2 1AQ
Tel: (031) 556 7171

Association of British Insurers
Aldermary House
Queen Street
London EC4N 1TT
Tel: (01) 248 4477

Association of British Travel
Agents (ABTA)
55-57 Newman Street
London W1P 4AH
Tel: (01) 637 2444

Association of Certified
Accountants
29 Lincoln's Inn Fields
London WC2A 3EE
Tel: (01) 242 6855

Association of Investment Trust
Companies
6th Floor Park House
16 Finsbury Circus
London EC2M 7JP
Tel: (01) 588 5347

Association of Mail Order
Publishers
1 New Burlington Street
London W1X 1FD
Tel: (01) 437 0706

Banking Information Service
10 Lombard Street
London EC3V 9AR
Tel: (01) 626 8486

Bank of England
Threadneedle Street
London EC2R 8AH
Tel: (01) 601 4444

Barclays Bank PLC
54 Lombard Street
London EC3P 3AH
Tel: (01) 636 1567

British Insurance & Investment
Brokers Association (BIBA)
14 Bevis Marks
London EC3A 7NT
Tel: (01) 623 9043

British Merchant Banking and
Securities Houses Association
Granite House
101 Cannon Street
London EC4N 5BA
Tel: (01) 283 7332

Building Employers
Confederation
82 New Cavendish Street
London W1N 8AD
Tel: (01) 580 5588

Building Societies Association
3 Savile Row
London W1X 1AF
Tel: (01) 437 0655

Building Society Commission
15/17 Great Marlborough Street
London W1V 2AX
Tel: (01) 437 9992

Chartered Institute of Arbitrators
75 Cannon Street
London EC4N 5BH
Tel: (01) 236 8761

Chartered Institute of Public Finance and Accountancy
1 Buckingham Place
London SW1E 6HS

CCN Systems Ltd
Talbot House
Talbot Street
Nottingham NG1 5HS
Tel: 0602-410888

Citizens' Advice Bureaux (National Association)
115-123 Pentonville Road
London N1 9L2
Tel: (01) 833 2181

Company Pensions Information Centre
7 Old Park Lane
London W1Y 3LJ
Tel: (01) 409 1933

Consumers' Association
14 Buckingham Street
London WC2N 6DS
Tel: (01) 839 1222

Corporation of Insurance and Financial Advisers (CIFA)
6/7 Leapale Road
Guildford
Surrey GU1 4JX
Tel: (0483) 39121

Inland Revenue
Somerset House
Strand
London WC2R 1LB
Tel: (01) 438 6622

Institute of Chartered Accountants in England and Wales
Chartered Accountants Hall
Moorgate Place
London EC2P 2BJ
Tel: (01) 628 7060

Institute of Chartered Accountants of Scotland
27 Queen Street
Edinburgh EH2 1LA
Tel: (031) 225 5673

Institute of Cost and Management Accountants
63 Portland Place
London W1N 4AB
Tel: (01) 580 6542

Institute of Chartered Secretaries and Administrators
16 Park Crescent
London W1N 4AH
Tel: (01) 580 4741

Institute of Insurance Consultants
PO Box 231
121A Queensway, Bletchley,
Milton Keynes MK1 1X2
Tel: (0908) 643364

Insurance Brokers Registration Council
15 St. Helens Place
London EC3A 6DS
Tel: (01) 588 4387

Department of Trade and Industry
1 Victoria Street
London SW1H 0ET
Tel: (01) 215 7877

Financial Intermediaries, Managers and Brokers Regulatory Association (FIMBRA)
22 Great Tower Street
London EC3R 5AQ
Tel: (01) 283 4814

Finance Houses Association
18 Upper Grosvenor Street
London W1X 9PB
Tel: (01) 491 2783

Incorporated Society of Valuers and Auctioneers
3 Cadogan Gate
London SW1X 0AS
Tel: (01) 235 2282

Industrial Life Offices Association
Aldermary House
10-15 Queen Street
London EC4N 1TL
Tel: (01) 248 4477

International Securities Regulatory Organisation (ISRO)
2nd Floor 45 London Wall
London EC2M 5TE
Tel: (01) 256 8823

Investment Management Regulatory Organisation (IMRO)
45 London Wall
London EC2M 5TE
Tel: (01) 256 7261

Land Registry
32 Lincoln's Inn Fields
London WC2A 3PH
Tel: (01) 405 3488

Law Society
113 Chancery Lane
London WC2A 1PL
Tel: (01) 242 1222

Life Assurance and Unit Trust Regulatory Organisation (LAUTRO)
Centre Point
103 New Oxford Street
London WC1A 1QH
Tel: (01) 379 0444

Life Insurance Association
Citadel House
Station Approach
Chorleywood
Herts
Tel: (09278) 5333

Lloyds Bank PLC
71 Lombard Street
London EC3P 3BS
Tel: (01) 626 1500

Mail Order Traders Association
25 Castle Street
Liverpool 2
Tel: (051) 227 4181

Midland Bank PLC
Poultry
London EC2P 2BX
Tel: (01) 606 9911

National Association of Conveyancers
2 Chichester Rents
40 Chancery Lane
London WC2A 1EG
Tel: (01) 404 5737

National Association of Estate Agents
21 Jury Street
Warwick CV34 4EH
Tel: (0926) 496800

National Association of Pension Funds
12-18 Grosvenor Gardens
London SW1W 0DH
Tel: (01) 730 0585

National Girobank
Bridle Road
Bootle
Merseyside G1R 0AA
Tel: (051) 928 8181

National House Building Council
58 Portland Place
London W1N 4BU
Tel: (01) 637 1248

Newspaper Publishers' Association Ltd.
6 Bouverie Street
London EC4Y 8OY
Tel: (01) 583 8132

National Westminster Bank PLC
41 Lothbury
London EC2P 2BP
Tel: (01) 606 6060

Newspaper Society
Whitefriar House
6 Carmelite Street
London EC4Y 0BL
Tel: (01) 583 3311

Occupational Pensions Advisory Service
Room 327, Aviation House
129 Kingsway
London WC2B 6NN
Tel:

Occupational Pensions Board
Lynwood Road
Thames Ditton
Surrey KT7 0DP
Tel: (01) 398 4242

Office of Fair Trading
Field House
15-25 Bream's Buildings
London EC4A 1PR
Tel: (01) 242 2858

Personal Insurance Arbitration Service
75 Cannon Street
London EC4N 5BH
Tel: (01) 236 8761

Royal Institute of British Architects (RIBA)
66 Portland Place
London W1N 4AD
Tel: (01) 580 5533

Royal Institute of Chartered Surveyors (RICS)
12 Great George Street
Parliament Square
London SW1P 3AD
Tel: (01) 222 7000

Securities and Investment
Board (SIB)
3 Royal Exchange Buildings
London EC3V 3NL
Tel: (01) 283 2474

Society of Pension Consultants
Ludgate House
Ludgate Circus
London EC4A 2AB
Tel: (01) 353 1688

Solicitors Complaints Bureau
Stock Exchange
Old Broad Street
London EC2N 1HP
Tel: (01) 834 2288

Trustee Savings Bank
PO Box 41
49-53 Surrey Row
London SE1 0BY
Tel: (01) 633 9344

Unit Trust Association
Park House
16 Finsbury Circus
London EC2M 7JP
Tel: (01) 628 0871

United Association for the
Protection of Trade (UAPT)
Zodiac House
163 London Road
Croydon
Tel: (01) 686 5644

OMBUDSMEN

Parliamentary Commissioner
and Health Service
Commissioner
Church House
Great Smith Street
London SW1P 3BW
Tel: (01) 212 7676

Insurance Ombudsman Bureau
31 Southampton Row
London WC1B 5HJ
Tel: (01) 242 8613

Building Society Ombudsman
Grosvenor Gardens House
Grosvenor Gardens
London SW1X 7AW
Tel: (01) 931 0044

Commissioners for Local
Administration
Greater London, South East,
South West, W. Midlands,
East Anglia
21 Queen Anne's Gate
London SW1H 9BU
Tel: (01) 222 5622

North and East Midlands
29 Castlegate
York YO1 1RN
Tel: (0904) 30151

Scotland
5 Shandwick Place
Edinburgh EH2 4RG
Tel: (031) 229 4472

Wales
Derwen House
Court Road
Bridgend
Mid-Glamorgan CF31 1BN
Tel: (0656) 61325

Office of the Banking
Ombudsman
Citadel House
5/11 Fetter Lane
London EC4A 1BR
Tel: (01) 583 1395